ANCIENT HAWAI'I

THE DISCOVERY OF OʻAHU
(A painting of three panels including the preceding page)
Collection of the Outrigger Waikiki Hotel

ANCIENT HAWAI'I

words and images by
HERB KAWAINUI KĀNE

The Kawainui Press
Captain Cook, Hawai'i 96704-0163

PRONUNCIATION

To readers who have not heard the spoken language, Hawaiian words can be as daunting as shoals to a sailor in uncharted waters. This guide does not address all the intricacies, but it may help you sound your way.

Every syllable ends with a vowel, and every vowel is sounded.

The ʻokina (ʻ) is a glottal stop, like the sound between the two oh's in the English oh-oh. In some words it marks where a consonant has been dropped from the ancient Polynesian language.

Stress (or accent) all vowels marked with macrons: ā, ē, ī, ō, ū.

When pronouncing combined vowels (ae. ai, ao, au, ei, eu, oi, ou) stress the first vowel and glide to the next. *Eu* will sound *ay-oo*. Aia will sound *ai-ya*.

Most words accent the next to last syllable and alternating preceding syllables: *HA-ma-KU-a*. On words with five syllables, accent the first and fourth syllable: *KU-ku-i-PA-hu*.

Vowel sounds:　*a* as *a* in above; or if stressed, as in far

　　　　　　e as *e* in bet; or if stressed, as ay in day

　　　　　　i as y in happy, or if stressed, as ee in see

　　　　　　o as the o in sole

　　　　　　u as the oo in moon

Consonants are the same as in English except for *w,* which is as in English, except after *i* and *e* when it is sounded as *v.* Before and after an *a* it's sometimes sounded as *v.*

The binding of this book is strengthened for school and library use by smyth-sewing.
All *kapa* reproduced in this book are copyrighted © by *kapa* artist Puanani Kanemura Van Dorpe
The paintings were photographed by Lee Allen Thomas, Maui Custom Color and Colorprints. Inc.
Color scanning by Steven Gray, Todd Olson, Aaron Shimakura
Pagemaker 6.5 assembly by James Raschick
Printed in China

CONTENTS

The eleven paintings cited in the Contents were an assignment from the Hualalai Development Company, builders of the Four Seasons Resort, Hualalai, at Ka'ūpūlehu in North Kona, on the Island of Hawai'i, where the paintings are on permanent display.

DEPENDENT AS WE ARE UPON MODERN TECHNOLOGY, WHAT MAY interest us most about ancient Pacific Islanders is how they accomplished so much with so little. We may call them "stone age," for they had no metals. We may call them "pre-literate," for they had no alphabet. The Arabic system of numbers and the invention of the wheel did not reach them. On islands without clays, the pottery skill of their Proto-Polynesian ancestors was forgotten. Yet without much of what we regard as essential to modern life, with only the meager material resources of their environment, they explored Earth's largest ocean and progressed beyond mere survival to build a culture of surprising affluence and complexity.

Much that we would like to know about them has been lost by the impact of Western ways as well as their own customs of secrecy. Much of what remains is tantalizingly indistinct, blurred through the lens of our modern vision, distorted by the fantasies and embellishments all peoples invent about their pasts.

Enough is known, however, as hard evidence or as conjecture carefully grounded on widely accepted cultural facts, to provide us with a view of a civilization that now seems alien and remote. Yet in their stories we hear themes that are hauntingly familiar, universal to other indigenous cultures throughout the world and archetypal to our own.

This little book is an introduction to a people who, aware of no others, knew themselves not as Hawaiians but simply as The People (Kānaka Maoli). Their 19th century descendants, buffeted by the impacts of Western culture, looked back to them wistfully as The People of Old (Ka Poʻe Kahiko). With the passage of another century they have become ever more distant from us, our view of their world increasingly obscured.

It was a world forever lost when waves of change began to crash against these shores.

Facing Page: COUNCIL OF CHIEFS

THE DISCOVERERS OF HAWAI'I

THEY CAME IN DOUBLE CANOES, SEARCHING NORTHWARD INTO AN unknown sea. Sailing on strange winds, paddling through doldrum calms, braving high seas and storms, they persisted in their quest for new land.

Behind them lay the South Pacific islands their ancestors had discovered centuries earlier. Observing plover and other shore birds flocking together each spring and migrating northward, they may have concluded that land lay in that direction.

Their spaceship was the voyaging canoe. Built with tools of stone, bone, and shell, assembled with lashings of braided fiber, and powered by sails of plaited matting, it was the finest product of any culture that knew no metals.

In these unfamiliar northern latitudes they were buffeted by strong prevailing easterly winds. When seas came over the gunwales, they bailed. When gusts ripped the sails, they made repairs. Lashings loosened by pounding waves were tightened or replaced. When drinking water and food supplies dwindled, they went on scant rations. And they endured.

For these were the Children of Tangaroa, Spirit of the Sea, and of Tāne, Tū, Rongo, mighty Spirits of Nature and the most senior ancestors of the People as well as all other beings in the universe. While other

explorers sailed with the comforting presence of continental coasts on their beam, Polynesians faced the open ocean without fear as their own and only world.

The moaning of conch shell trumpets kept canoes together at night. Sailing under the rising stars of the northern sky, reaching across powerful Northeast Tradewinds, they came upon a chain of islands of immense size. They searched for a landing; and when their canoes touched shore, human history in Hawai'i had begun.

Their landing, we may believe, was not made without some ceremony to placate the spirits of this strange new land. They planted the cuttings, tubers and seeds they had carefully protected from seawater. Until their first harvest was ready they subsisted by fishing, bird hunting, and gathering. And, over many generations, they made these islands a Polynesian place.

We know nothing of their traditions, nor the names by which they knew themselves or these islands. The traditions we know as Hawaiian originated with others from the South Pacific who came to rule them centuries later. But we know from the archaeological record that they were Polynesian.

A thousand years would pass before the Vikings of another ocean would dare venture away from Europe's shores.

ORIGINS

WHENCE THE POLYNESIANS? THEIR LANGUAGE, ANIMALS AND plants bespeak an ancient origin in Southeast Asia, where a native people may have been displaced by more powerful neighbors and forced to take to the sea, developing a maritime culture as they moved eastward through the many islands of what is now Indonesia. Archaeologists have found distinctive "Lapita" pottery 4,000 years old, and fragments of obsidian possibly 6,000 years old, marking a 2,300 mile "voyaging corridor" from Borneo eastward along the northern shore of New Guinea to the Admiralty Islands and New Britain in Melanesia—evidence of a people with seafaring skills superior to those of the present inhabitants.

Melanesia had been inhabited by dark-skinned peoples long before their arrival, New Guinea for more than 30,000 years. We may call the newcomers Proto-Polynesians, a people changing culturally and physically, becoming but not yet Polynesian. Although they shared a culture, they may have lived in many groups, some exploring northward into the area of small islands now known as Micronesia and contributing to the ancestry of Micronesians, others acquiring Melanesian genes during periods of settlement along the northern coast of New Guinea or in the many islands of Melanesia. The trail of Lapita pottery leads eastward to Fiji, apparently settled by a people of mixed Proto-Polynesian and Melanesian ancestry.

Searching farther to the east, others found uninhabited islands in Sāmoa—where finds of pottery are 3,000 years old—and Tonga. Here in this "Cradle of Polynesia," perhaps no more than a few canoe loads of Proto-Polynesians arrived. Over centuries they evolved the distinctive

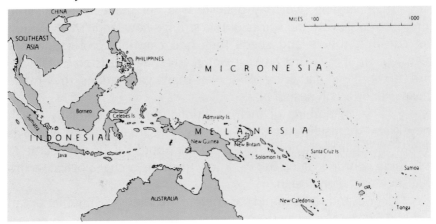

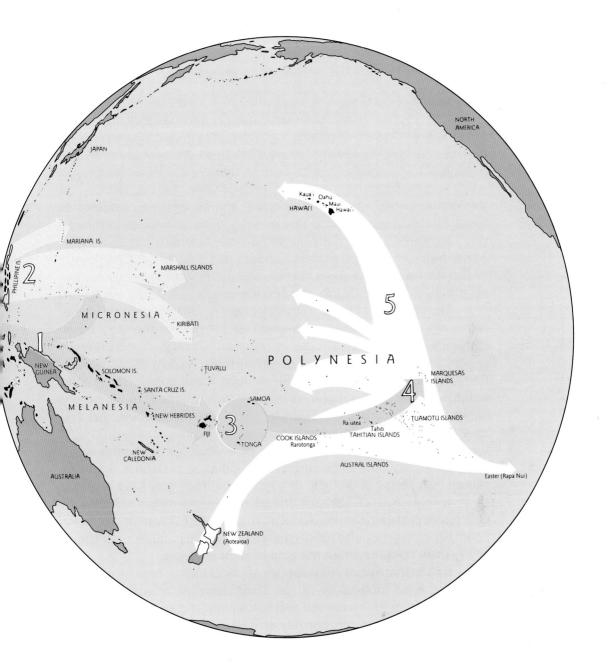

1. The ancient route from Asia by way of Indonesia and Melanesia of ancestors of Polynesians Some may have turned northward into Micronesia (small islands). Melanesia (black islands) was settled many thousands of years earlier by dark-skinned peoples.

2. Micronesia received voyagers from Asia by way of the Philippines.

3. Discovered more than 3,000 years ago, Sāmoa, Tonga and the eastern islands of Fiji became the "Cradle of Polynesia," where distinctive Polynesian physical and cultural traits evolved within an originally small group.

4. Polynesians reached the Marquesas, and possibly the Tahitian Islands.

5. Archaeological findings suggest that "Eastern," or "Marginal" Polynesia was explored from the Marquesas and possibly Tahiti, by canoes sailing north to Hawai'i (about 2,000 years ago), east to Easter Island, and southwest to the Cook Islands and New Zealand.

physical and cultural traits now regarded as Polynesian.

Later explorations continued the habit of moving eastward. Unable to sail against the prevailing easterly winds, they would have waited for periods of unsettled weather when wind shifts, brought about by the passage of low pressure troughs, enabled them to make their easting on winds varying from the north, west, or south. The Tahitian Islands and the Marquesas Islands were discovered, and became new homelands which spawned explorations to the outer limits of Polynesia. Hawai'i was discovered to the north at some time before 1,900 years ago, Easter Island (Rapa Nui) to the southeast, and New Zealand (Aotearoa) to the southwest—the three corners of a triangle equal in size to the combined surfaces of North and South America.

The discovery of Hawai'i could not have resulted from an accidental drift voyage of helpless storm-wrecked fishermen; the way north demanded close-reaching against the wind through three different regions of prevailing winds and ocean currents. A coconut cannot drift from the South Pacific to Hawai'i through these zones. Those who sailed were on a purposeful voyage of exploration. They knew the dangers; they knew of canoes which had sailed and never returned; but their ancestors had always found new islands in their ocean world, and the spirits of their most powerful ancestors would guide them now.

They may have been driven by population pressures, a famine caused by a period of drought, or a lost battle. They may have been led by an ambitious chief, perhaps one whose older brothers had left him with few expectations at home. Not all voyages were driven by necessity. South Pacific legends also tell of explorations made purely for adventure or to satisfy curiosity about the girls of another island.

No less than twenty four species of plants upon which their culture depended were brought by canoe. Their domestic animals were the pig, a chicken of iridescent red and black plumage, and a small dog. A species of small black rat probably arrived as a stowaway.

These plants and animals were of a Southeast Asian origin with the exception of the sweet potato. Believed to be of South American origin, its wide distribution in Polynesia suggests that it arrived at a very early time. The Polynesian term for sweet potato, *kumara,*is also a Peruvian Indian term (in Hawaiian *kumara* has become *'uala*). Whether it was brought by Indians on a raft, or as a prize taken home by early Polynesian explorers, we will never know. The raft theory, launched by Thor Heyerdahl's *Kon Tiki* voyage, involves a one-way trip and may seem the most economical. But Indians were accustomed to sailing within the comforting presence of a continent. Those on a raft blown out to sea would have struggled to get back to land, no doubt consuming any vegetable on board. Polynesians were open-ocean sailors, knowing only islands, and accustomed to conserving rations and protecting plants from seawater over long voyages.

South of Easter Island an exploring canoe might find winds upon which to reach eastward. Beyond Easter Island, winds and current begin a long curve toward the northeast that would carry a canoe to Peru. Off Peru, the current wheels to the northwest under the Southeast Tradewinds. With such prevailing winds, a swift canoe might sail to Peru and return to Polynesia in less time than a raft could sail one way.

Wherever Polynesians explored and established new settlements, they carried an ancient memory of an original homeland in the west. The name, Havaiki, may refer to Savai'i in Sāmoa, or some place farther west. It was given to Havai'i (later Ra'iatea), and Hawai'i. After death, many believed their spirits would leap from the westernmost point of their island and fly back to the ancient homeland of their ancestors.

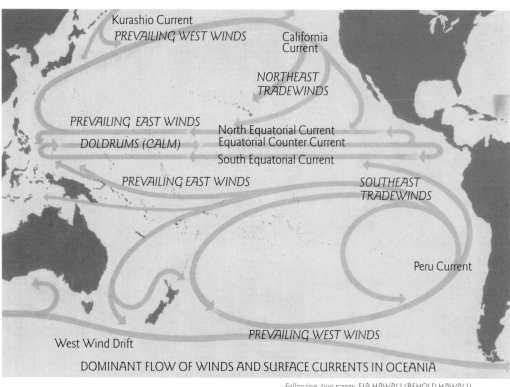

Kurashio Current
PREVAILING WEST WINDS
California Current
NORTHEAST TRADEWINDS
PREVAILING EAST WINDS
DOLDRUMS (CALM)
North Equatorial Current
Equatorial Counter Current
South Equatorial Current
PREVAILING EAST WINDS
SOUTHEAST TRADEWINDS
Peru Current
West Wind Drift
PREVAILING WEST WINDS

DOMINANT FLOW OF WINDS AND SURFACE CURRENTS IN OCEANIA

Following two pages: EIA HAWAI'I (BEHOLD HAWAI'I)
Collection of Michael and Diane McLean

TAHITIAN CONQUEST

Of THE FIRST HAWAIIANS, WE KNOW ONLY THAT THEY WERE Polynesians, possibly from the Marquesas Islands two thousand miles away, and we know them only through archaeology. Their names and traditions are lost, obliterated by high status chiefs who arrived perhaps a thousand years later from the leeward Tahitian islands of Ra'iatea, Bora Bora and Huahine. With these new rulers the Hawaiian traditions begin. Histories are composed by conquerors.

Ra'iatea had become a powerful center of cultural change, and its major temple, Taputapuatea, a "Vatican" from which chiefs derived great *mana* and status. They adventured and conquered in all directions. On the Island of Tahiti they fought and subjugated people they called Manahune. In Hawaiian tradition, Menehune probably derives from the same term given to the original inhabitants of the Hawaiian Islands.

The term is disparaging, belittling, meaning a people of small status. But when Western writers heard stories of Menehune, they thought their informants were speaking of a people of small size. European tales of leprechauns and gnomes leaped to mind, imaginations took wing, and a new genre of "Hawaiian" folk-lore was born—no doubt abetted by Hawaiian informants as soon as they perceived the joke and revised their stories accordingly. Writers received tales of a magically strong little folk working in great numbers, building great voyaging canoes, huge temple platforms, long aqueducts and large fishponds—each project completed in a single night or left undone. There is, however, no authentic Hawaiian tradition of the Menehune as a race of physically small people.

On Kaua'i you may see solid evidence of an earlier people: the rockwork lining the "Menehune ditch"—an ancient aqueduct that once brought water from the Waimea river to irrigate dry lands for growing taro. The rocks were shaped and fitted together—a method of stonework requiring immense labor, and not typical of Hawaiian rockwork. At Nawiliwili the large Alekoko fishpond is said to have been built by Menehune.

A retreat by Menehune groups along the island chain would explain why the island of Kaua'i, as their last holdout, has the most stories about them. Tales of the Menehune as a people living in the mountains but with a taste for seafood suggest they had been driven inland from the shore. It is also said that the Menehune king at last gave it up and sailed off to the west with most of his people. They would have passed

1. Voyagers sailing from Western Polynesia, exploring to the west on the prevailing easterly winds, settled on islands in Southern Micronesia and Eastern Melanesia, now known as the Polynesian outliers. Samoan voyagers were ancestors of some Cook Island clans. From the 17th century into the 19th century, Tongans regularly visited Samoa, raided north through Tuvalu and into Micronesian Kiribati, and fought as mercenaries in Fiji.

2. About 1,000 years ago the leeward Tahitian islands (Ra'iatea, Bora Bora, and Huahine) became a center of cultural change and great *mana* from which adventurous high-status chiefs sailed to establish their rule in Tahiti and in the Hawaiian, Cook, Austral, and Tuamotu Islands. Some clans emigrated to New Zealand, which may have been rediscovered during this era. Hawaiian traditions begin with this era of conquest; those of earlier Polynesian inhabitants were not preserved.

Necker Island stone images may have been made by early settlers. Not Hawaiian in style, they resemble Marquesan stone carvings.

Facing page: OLOPANA: A chief of Waipi'o Valley, Hawai'i, Olopana led a voyage to "Tahiti of the Golden Haze," the first in a saga of ancient voyages spanning three generations. *Collection of the Kaua'i Coconut Beach Hotel, Kaua'i*

Necker and Nihoa islands, where carved stone images have been found which are Polynesian but not typically Hawaiian. But some apparently remained on Kaua'i, where a census ordered by King Kaumuali'i in the early 19th century recorded 65 persons as being of Menehune ancestry.

After voyaging was opened from the Tahitian leeward islands there arrived in Hawai'i the high priest Pā'ao. Here he determined that the chiefs, by intermarriage with lower classes, had lost the purity of lineage necessary to receive chiefly *mana* from the patron spirits. By his standards, none were qualified to rule. Back he sailed to his homeland, where he recruited Pili, a prince of the purest lineage. Returning to Hawai'i, no doubt with a strong force, Pā'ao installed Pili as king, and Pili founded the dynasty from which Kamehameha descended 28 generations later. Pā'ao instituted new rites and built temples. At about the time William the Conqueror crossed the English Channel, Pā'ao logged not less than 9,000 miles on his three voyages.

Breadfruit may not have reached Hawai'i until this era. In Polynesia the tree has been under cultivation so long that it will not seed itself, but must be transplanted as a sprout from the root of a parent tree, and is often difficult to move successfully from one yard to the next. That it could be brought three thousand miles in an open canoe is evidence of the horticultural skills of ancient planters. A legend of this time credits Kaha'i, a grandson of Mo'ikeha, for bringing breadfruit from Taha'a (then Upolu), a small island at the northern end of the Ra'iatea lagoon in the leeward Tahitian islands .

Voyaging between Hawai'i and the South Pacific appears to have ceased several centuries before European arrival. No explanation is found in the traditions, but several may be imagined. The appropriation and development of lands much larger than any they had known in the South Pacific demanded much attention, leaving little time for voyaging. Those who visited their southern homelands may have found that shifting alliances had made them less welcome; and, in the murky world of chiefly politics, there was always the danger that a chief who went on a long voyage might return to find his place usurped by another.

NAVIGATORS

In 1769, at Tahiti, Captain James Cook took aboard H.M.S. *Endeavor* the navigator Tupaia, who guided Cook 300 miles south to the island of Rurutu. The expedition sailed westward on various courses to New Zealand, then to Australia, then northward through the Great Barrier Reef, touching at New Guinea. Throughout this entire convoluted voyage, Cook was astonished to discover that whenever Tupaia was asked to point out the direction in which Tahiti lay, he could do so without access to the ship's charts or compass. The experiment ended when the expedition reached Batavia in the Dutch East Indies, where malaria and dysentery killed Tupaia and many of *Endeavor's* crew.

Today, our perceptions dulled by dependence on instruments, feats such as Tupaia's—based on a sensitivity which comes from living intimately with nature—seem incredible. But Cook was convinced that among the Polynesians were navigators capable of guiding canoes over great distances.

A brotherhood of experts trained to acute powers of observation and memory, Polynesian navigators were also priests responsible for conducting the rituals of their profession and invoking spiritual help. Whereas the modern navigator is equipped to fix his position without reference to his place of departure, the Polynesian used a system that was home-oriented. He kept a mental record of all courses steered and all phenomena affecting the movement of the canoe, tracing these backwards in his mind so that at any time he could point in the approximate direction of his home island and estimate the sailing time required to reach it—a complex feat of dead reckoning. This required careful attention. It also meant insufficient sleep. It's been said that the navigator could always be distinguished among his companions on a canoe by his bloodshot eyes.

After the discovery of a new island, the altitude of stars passing overhead and the places on the horizon of rising and setting stars would be carefully observed and incorporated into the lore of the navigators. Such knowledge would enable them to find the island again. Places for astronomical study were built, often as rock platforms oriented in some relationship to certain celestial events.

By aligning a canoe with landmarks, departing canoes could set out upon known courses. The rising and setting places of familiar stars provided a compass. Knowledge of the paths of such stars rising or setting in succession enabled navigators to steer on bearings which had

Facing Page: NAVIGATOR *(KAHUNA KILO HŌKŪ) Collection of Stephen and Diane Heiman*

been worked out from experience. When stars were obscured, dominant ocean swells, marching consistently across vast areas, were dependable direction indicators. The presence of low islands might be detected by clouds building in rising warm air and appearing stationary while smaller clouds drift with the wind. Over atolls, clouds may reflect the green of sunlit lagoons. Other indicators of low islands below the horizon were reflected ocean swells interrupting the dominant swells of the open ocean, drifting flotsam and the daily flights of shore-based birds seeking fish as far as thirty miles from home. Island groups presented larger, safer targets than isolated islands; once a landfall was made at any island in a known group, the canoe could be sailed to a specific island.

NAVIGATOR ON THE OBSERVATORY
Collection of Sandra and William Gray

The zenith stars of an island are those which appear to pass directly overhead, such as Hōkūleʻa (Arcturus) for Hawaiʻi and ʻAʻā (Sirius) for Tahiti. On a voyage from Tahiti to Hawaiʻi, the navigator would first be concerned with making sufficient easting to arrive at the latitude of Hawaiʻi upwind of his objective; then, when Hōkūleʻa appeared to arch directly overhead, the canoe could be turned downwind, and sailed directly westward to Hawaiʻi. If there were any uncertainty of latitude, the canoe could be sailed in long downwind tacks to expand its landfinding range. After an arduous voyage, the name Hōkūleʻa (star of gladness) is most appropriate as a star that leads to a happy landing.

Such basic principles are much easier to express in words than in practice. On its 1995 return voyage the canoe replica *Hōkūleʻa* sailed northward under heavy clouds which concealed the stars. Only a very brief sighting of Hōkūpaʻa (Polaris) was made. Its altitude above the horizon informed the navigators that they had arrived at the approximate latitude of Hawaiʻi. They turned the canoe downwind, and two nights later saw the glow of the lights of the town of Hilo.

There was, in addition to knowledge gained by training and practical experience, evidence of a special talent which transcends conscious reasoning and enters the realm of the intuitive. Incidents have been recorded of landfalls accurately predicted by Polynesian sailors aboard European vessels after overcast skies or accidents had caused uncertainty about the ships' positions.

All sailors learn that success is possible only by trimming sails and ship to a dynamic balance with natural forces. It was a lesson not lost on the Polynesians, whose survival on land as well as at sea depended upon maintaining an equilibrium with nature.

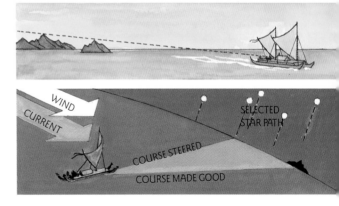

LANDMARKS: Departing at sunset, navigators set their course to a known destination by alignment with landmarks. The drift of the vessel from that alignment might indicate the direction and strength of the current. later, he may pick up his bearing from a familiar star.

STAR PATHS: On east-west courses navigators steered toward stars known to rise or set over their destination. Steering was adjusted to compensate for the leeway (sideways drift) caused by the wind and current, the angle estimated from experience. To maintain this angle they guided on stars dead ahead, replacing them with others in the same path as the guiding stars rose too high to be useful or set below the horizon.

PITCHING   ROLLING   BOTH MOTIONS

OCEAN SWELLS: Prevailing winds or storms generate swells which pulse across the ocean for thousands of miles. Under overcast skies navigators could maintain their heading by keeping a constant ratio between the amount of pitching or rolling induced by a dominant swell, holding direction until guiding stars became visible again.

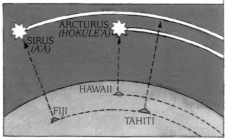

ZENITH STARS for an island are those which seem to pass directly overhead. Such stars also appear to pass directly overhead on the same latitude at any position east or west of that island. On north-south courses, a navigator who kept upwind of his destination until its zenith star was overhead could then turn downwind to make a landfall. The range of visual sighting could be broadened by taking wide tacks downwind. *Hōkūleʻa* (Arcturus) is a zenith star for Hawaiʻi Island. *Aʻa* (Sirius) is a zenith star for Tahiti and Fiji.

FISHING BIRDS heading out to sea at dawn or returning at dusk point the direction to their home islands. CUMULUS CLOUDS generated by warm updrafts may rise high above an island, appearing stationary while fragments of the main cloud and scattered cumulus clouds drift away in the wind.

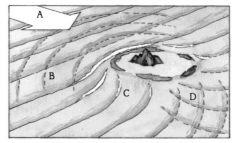

SEA COLOR: A color change from the deep blue of the open sea to green may betray a familiar reef, enabling navigators to check their position. FLOTSAM: Drifting wood or leaves betray land to windward, and drifting seaweed may indicate an upcurrent reef. A greenish tinge to the underside of a cloud reflects sunlight from a distant lagoon too far away to be seen.

SWELL PATTERNS: A dominant swell bounces back from an island and bends around it, creating swell patterns which can be read to find an unseen landfall. (A) main swell; (B) reflected swell; (C) refracted swell; (D) shadow of turbulence.

ISLAND GROUPS (below): Signs of unseen land expand low or obscured island targets by 25 to 30 miles. In island groups these extensions often overlap, forming broad targets. To find an island within a group, voyagers could aim for the approximate center of the group, then change course to their specific destination after sighting a familiar island. Sailing from Ra'iatea to Rarotonga, navigators sighting any known landfall in the Cook Islands chain could then sail to a position for an accurate course to Rarotonga..

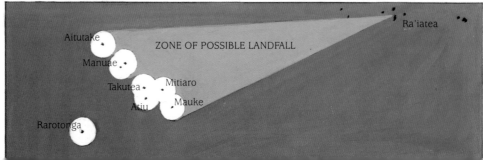

ZONE OF POSSIBLE LANDFALL

Ra'iatea
Aitutake
Manuae
Takutea
Mitiaro
Atiu
Mauke
Rarotonga

POLYNESIAN GENESIS

In the beginning there was only darkness, an infinite and timeless night. But within that void brooded an intelligence. The Earth Mother, Papa, was created in the darkness. Light was created—the procreative light of the Sky Father, Wākea. In their embrace male light penetrated female darkness, and from this union of opposites was created a universe of opposites.

So it was that the Universe was given form and life; for only in the union of light and darkness can there be life and growth of living things, all fathered by sunlight and mothered in the darkness of the soil, the egg or the womb.

The great spirits were born. Tāne the Creator was the first born, and as the eldest he reigned over the others. He was the spirit of creation, of sunlight, fresh water, and forests, and the male ancestor of all living things, including The People.

There was Tangaroa of the Ocean; and Tū, who in many guises and under many names was patron of the works of men; and Rongo, patron of agriculture and healing. These were the male ancestors of all things in nature, the sources of all power, or *mana*. When these spirits came to Hawai'i there was a great turbulence of thunderstorms and whirlwinds and blazes of lightning. Their eyes flashed upon the land and the earth shook as they landed upon it.

In the evolution of the Hawaiian language their names would change to Kāne, Kanaloa, Kū, and Lono.

Also born was the supreme female spirit, known as Hina in some manifestations and as Haumea in others. Heir to the power of creation, patroness of women's works, she is mother of many spirits. As La'ila'i (tranquility), Haumea was the mother of the first humans. Continually reshaping herself by rebirth, she retreats in old age to the spirit world, then reappears as a desirable young woman, taking many husbands among successive generations of her children and grandchildren. As Hina, she is associated with darkness, in some stories emerging from the ocean depths as a beautiful woman, in others escaping from the cruelties of life into the night sky where she can be seen against the full moon beating *kapa*. Pele, spirit of volcanoes, was born to Haumea in the ancient homeland, and voyaged to Hawai'i with sisters and brothers in a great canoe, guided by an elder brother in the form of a shark.

These greatest of spirits were ancestors of the People and of all life, and in this way the people were related to all other living things. In the time of the People such spirits have been invisible, appearing only through the many manifestations of their *mana*.

Mana was the invisible force that flowed from the most senior spirits to energize everything in the universe, whether it be the wind, the growth of a plant, or the surge of an ocean wave. *Mana* became manifest in humans as outstanding talents, intelligence, strengths, and leadership charisma. *Tapu* (Hawaiian: *kapu*) were prohibitions instituted to protect the flow of *mana* from disruption and conserve it against accidental loss or theft by persons not entitled to it. Today the meaning of *tapu* is largely confined to signs warning against trespassing, but the terms *mana* and *tapu* (as taboo) have entered the English language.

PELE'S VOYAGE FROM THE ANCIENT HOMELAND
Collection of William and Kahala Ann Trask-Gibson

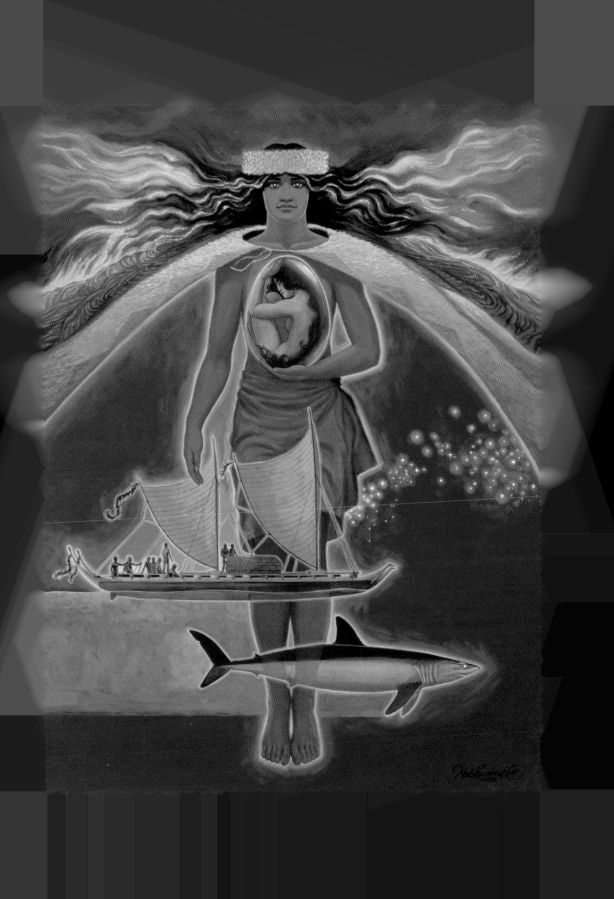

MOMENT OF CONTACT: The Cook Expedition off Kaua'i, 1778
Collection of the Kauai Marriott Resort

WORLDS APART

WHEN THE BRITISH EXPEDITION UNDER CAPTAIN JAMES COOK arrived in Hawai'i, differences of world view and logic between the two cultures often made actions which were perfectly rational to one group seem bizarre or incomprehensible to the other. Hawai'i was not unique; throughout the world, wherever the emerging modern European culture collided with a culture rooted in a primal past, the same gulf of misunderstanding existed.

As the myths of Polynesia reveal, the lives from which these stories arose were radically different from our own. But only nine centuries earlier Cook's Viking ancestors, whose Danelaw conquests extended from London to Scotland, were of a society essentially similar to that of the Polynesian Hawaiians. Students of Greek mythology and the Homeric tales also find striking similarities in Polynesian traditions—

the same gifting and endless feasting as affirmations of status, the same clan loyalties suppressing feelings of individuality, the same ruling aristocracy of hereditary chiefs (*hero* in Greek, *ali'i* in Hawaiian). In Norse, Greek and Polynesian tales we find pantheons of gods reflecting human frailties as well as virtues. From native cultures throughout the world we hear the same stories with differences caused by different environments, a sameness which mythologists see as expressive of the nature of humanity.

If Cook's men and their Hawaiian hosts interpreted each others' behavior as strange, it was because each side viewed its world through different lenses. The disparity between European and Polynesian customs and attitudes had evolved from different basic premises about the universe and humanity's role within it. For example, after Cook tried to kidnap the Hawaiian king as a hostage against the return of a stolen—or impounded—boat and got himself killed by the king's bodyguards, and after an uneasy peace was restored, a Hawaiian asked the British when Cook might return, and what might he do to them. The question, taken by some Western scholars as evidence that Cook had been seen as a god, is simply explained by the Hawaiian belief in ghosts as spirits with powers of retribution. Different concepts, different lenses. By their own perceptions and reasoning the Hawaiians of Cook's time were intensely practical, as their survival in an environment without metals demanded. Today, bewildered by the logic of a culture radically different from our own, seekers of convenient explanations too often surround their perceptions of ancient ways with a romantic aura of mysticism and magic that never existed.

Europeans, heavily influenced by Judeo-Christian beliefs, saw the universe as two separate spheres, natural and supernatural, under one supernatural male creator, with selected humans (Christians) below the Supernatural in the hierarchy but elevated above, and given dominion over, Nature (everything else in the Universe, including other peoples). Such dominion logically included rights of conquest and exploitation. The journals of Western explorations from the 15th century well into the 19th century show that Europeans enjoyed the conceit that native peoples of other lands might see them as superior beings, if not as gods. Native awe at European technology was misinterpreted as recognition of an innate European superiority.

We look back on "the Dawn of Humanism" as a flowering of philosophy, the arts and sciences. More to the point, it was the individual's awakening to self awareness, and an emerging middle class striving to win, by purchase or politics, rights by which an individual could attend to his self interest. It was discovered that investment in science, technology and exploration could produce new inventions, new markets and greater profits.

After Galileo and Newton, the Western world view would be forever changed, with no turning back. When Cook reached Hawai'i, Europeans, in their "Age of Enlightenment" were beginning to replace their mythology of the past with a mythology of the future.

At that moment, individual rights incomprehensible a few centuries earlier were being asserted by the American Revolution as "self evident" and "inalienable." Individual rights expressed in initiative and self-service imparted a dynamism and audacity to Western culture that less resilient indigenous cultures could not withstand.

By contrast, Polynesians saw their universe as a perfect creation, eternal, with change limited to seasonal and life cycles—an organic whole of which each thing or person was an integral part. Natural or human disasters occurred when things got out of balance. Success depended upon living in accord with Nature's equilibrium, preserving the status quo as the spirits had created it.

Theirs was a universe of opposites—light and darkness, male and female, heat and cold, wetness and dryness, hardness and softness, growth and decay, roughness and smoothness—none of which can exist without its opposite.

Apparently there was no concept of the supernatural as a sphere separate from Nature. Polynesian religion was so integrated with life that no separate word for it was needed. The original creative spirits were their natural ancestors, as well as the progenitors of everything else in the universe. Humans and all other life forms were related by a common ancestry. The multitude of spirits of ancestors, of the forest, ocean, winds, mountains and volcanoes were viewed as natural rather than supernatural. If we take "god" to mean a supernatural being, the term mistranslates *akua*, which means a being of immense power, whether a spirit or a living person. Revering the original creators as their ultimate ancestors, Polynesians would have found the modern idea of a conquest of Nature to be incomprehensible, patricidal, and certain to bring terrible retribution from natural forces.

Moku (major districts)
of Hawai'i Island

THE LAND

Because Land Was Immortal And Humans Mortal, The Idea that humans could own land was beyond imagining. Their attitude was one of territorial custody rather than ownership. It was said that land could not belong to men because men belonged to the land.

In his 1840 Constitution of the Kingdom of Hawaii, Kamehameha III stated that although his father was the founder of the kingdom, the land *"...was not his own private property. It belonged to the chiefs and people in common, of whom Kamehameha I was the head, and had the management of the landed property."*

Eight years later, after American advisors convinced him that a distribution of land to his people would be humane and appropriate to the times, land ownership was instituted. Unaccustomed to the concept, many Hawaiians fell prey to acquisitive newcomers. But in most Pacific Islands today, most of the lands either cannot be bought by outsiders or may be purchased only under severe restrictions. In some island nations the lands remain largely under the control of the hereditary chiefs, now operating as trustees of native land trusts.

In old Hawai'i, kings awarded custody of lands to their loyal supporters. Island kingdoms *(mokupuni)* were divided into districts *(moku)* which were further parceled into minor chiefdoms *(ahupua'a)*. Because boundaries with neighboring *ahupua'a* were not crossed with impunity, these land divisions typically extended from the high forested mountains to offshore fishing grounds, providing the residents with access to the resources of all elevations without crossing borders. Within each *ahupua'a* were *'ili*, smaller holdings, each typically worked by one extended family.

The meaning of *ahupua'a* derives from altars *(ahu)* of rockwork marking the boundary of each *ahupua'a* where it was crossed by the main trail that circled the island. Wooden images of a pig *(pua'a)*, stained with red earth, were placed on these altars during the annual Makahiki tour, and to these were brought the annual taxes, a gifting of craftswork and foodstuffs ceremonially made to the chiefs. Throughout the Hawaiian Islands, the names of *moku* and some *ahupua'a* are preserved as geographic areas.

RULING CHIEFS

A paramount chief, or king* (*ali'i nui*) wears a feathered helmet (*mahiole*) and cloak (*'ahu'ula*). Full length cloaks were worn ceremonially; in battle, shorter capes were worn. The feathered *malo* worn around the waist and over the left shoulder signifies investiture as a king. Both figures wear carved whalestooth pendants on neckpieces of finely braided hair of ancestors (*lei niho palaoa*). An abstraction of a tongue, it signifies that the wearer speaks with authority. She wears a voluminous *kapa* wrap, a feathered head *lei*, a boar's tusk bracelet, and carries a small feathered *kāhili*, a fly whisk that evolved as a chiefly symbol.

The temple image at left is carved in a style typical of Hawai'i Island. Beneath the image the *kahuna nui*, high priest of Kū (patron spirit of the chiefs), holds a feathered spirit image wrapped in *kapa*. Beside the *kahuna nui* stands the *kālaimoku* (prime minister and chief diplomat), holding a stalk of *tī*, a sign of truce or peace. At right stands a servant, a guard bearing a feathered standard (*kāhili*) of a height that warns commoners of the king's approach, and an armed bodyguard. As in Europe, Hawaiian rulers often recruited sons of district chiefs for training in their court, a practice calculated to insure loyalty.

*"King," from the Old English "cyning" when there were many such worthies throughout Britain, was synonymous to "paramount chief" and is used here in that meaning.

Collection of The Four Seasons Resort, Hualalai

CHIEFS

THE ORAL HISTORY OF HAWAI'I BEFORE EUROPEAN CONTACT IS LARGELY composed of the the annals of the chiefs *(ali'i)*. Time was kept not by years but by generations; a memorable event would be marked as occurring "in the reign of" a certain king. The right of chiefly families to rule was based on a form of seniority—genealogies linking them as direct descendants of the major spirits. Through this genealogical connection *mana* flowed from the major spirits—benevolent ancestors— to the chiefs. It was said that in the beginning all the People could trace descent from these great spirits, but the families of commoners (*maka'āinana*) had long ago forgotten their genealogies, thereby losing the connection by which they might receive chiefly power. Different in formula, but similar to the concept of rule by divine right so popular with kings and emperors elsewhere.

Chiefs were ranked in several classes according to the lineage of each of their parents. Of the highest class were those whose lineages were most impeccable, believed to offer the least disruption to the flow of *mana* which descended to them from their patron spirits. This was *mana* of the chiefly kind, an invisible force flowing through the persons of men and women of perfect pedigree to benefit the entire community, manifesting as good governance, security, and prosperity for all. Where necessary, preservation of pedigree was achieved by brother and sister marriage. Not simply snobbery carried to the point of incest, such marriages were driven by the perceived need to keep the conduits for chiefly *mana* open.

Elaborate precautions were taken to guard a high-ranking bride until she became pregnant. Each night, chiefly witnesses guarded the marriage house, allowing no man but her husband to enter, forestalling any challenge against the lineage of the royal infant that might be brought later.

Chiefs of paramount rank were protected from situations which might cause them to lose *mana*, such as contact with commoners whose very proximity might drain *mana* from them. A commoner who stepped into the shadow of a such a chief committed a capital offense.

The king served as the interface between men and Kū, patron spirit of men's works, from whom flowed *mana* for governance, diplomacy, warfare, fishing, agriculture, public works, canoe building and other men's crafts. The most imposing temples *(heiau)* were the *luakini,* dedicated to Kū. Of all the spirits, only Kū merited that most precious gift, the life of a man, and only the king could order it.

From childhood, chiefs were trained to an ideal of the perfect chief, one who led and inspired his people by wise and courageous example. Chiefs might personally lead their commoners in heavy labor—planting, building fishponds, constructing rock platforms for temples—as well as in battle. However, just as European ideals of knighthood were often honored more by their breach than by observance, chiefly standards were sometimes disregarded when inconvenient. Those who behaved most outrageously may be most indelibly remembered, as they are in all histories, though probably far fewer in number than those who quietly and diligently strived to live a virtuous life.

At Right: KAMEHAMEHA BUILDING PU'UKOHOLĀ HEIAU
He is depicted as the tall figure facing the reader,
attended by a *kāhili* bearer and a guard with a spear,
and working in the line of men passing rocks.
Collection of the National Park Service

MANA AND RANK

Authority in Polynesia was based on seniority (inherited *mana*) and on acquired *mana* made evident by personal talents and accomplishments. Within an extended family (*'ohana*), consisting of everyone related by blood, marriage or adoption, younger members deferred to the superior mana and rank of elder siblings and to the authority of their parents (*mākua*). The *'ohana* also included spirits of venerated ancestors (*'aumākua*) to whom acts of respect were paid daily. Chiefly families ruled commoner families by genealogical seniority, claiming descent from the most senior and most powerful spirits (*akua*). Viewed as the natural order, compliance with the authority of one's elders was a rule seldom challenged.

If a man's accomplishments were greater than those of another of equal genealogical rank, his *mana* was greater. He would have authority over the other and receive more status and respect.

That's not to say he would have more freedom as an individual,

for with greater rank came a greater burden of responsibility for others. Unlike the modern society which values individuality and individual rights, Polynesians placed the clan's interest over self interest. Individual expression or initiative that did not contribute to the welfare of one's clan was discouraged if not punished. Indeed, there was little awareness of the individual self; in their thinking, "we" always came before "me."

It has not been unusual for a Westerner, after celebrating a satisfactory business agreement with a Polynesian, to learn with some dismay that the Polynesian's elder brother must now be consulted, then perhaps the father or an uncle.

There were traditional Polynesian ways of handling behavior problems and family disputes. A youngster who misbehaved and refused to conform would receive no further attention, but would be completely ignored, as if he or she did not exist. No word of response, no food or place to sleep could be offered to someone who did not exist. Such tentative banishment usually forced a quick return to acceptable behavior, for the loss of one's place within the clan meant loss of all benefits and protection. In Ancient Hawai'i, ostracism could be a death sentence.

Family disputes were—and often still are—resolved by the custom of *ho'opo-nopono* (to set things right). Guided by a clan elder whose *mana* and rank insure deference, disputing members join in expressions of *aloha* and praise for their beloved clan relatives. Holding fast to that spirit of accord and love, they are gently guided through stages of confession, remorse, repentance and reconciliation.

KAHUNA KĀLAI KI'I (the carver of images)
Collection of the Hawai'i State Foundation on Culture & the Arts

KĀHUNA

As LEADING EXPERTS, *KĀHUNA* WERE CULTURAL COUNTERPARTS of the guildmasters and priests of Mediæval Europe. Beyond serving as the leading practitioner of his craft or profession, each acted as an interface between his guild and its patron spirits. As the guildmaster represented his colleagues at the cathedral, praying to their patron saint for spiritual assistance, so did the *kahuna* perform rituals at temple or shrine to solicit *mana* from the patron spirits of his guild. As in Europe, a guild was often dominated by an extended family, but exceptionally talented novices from other families might gain admittance.

The *kahuna nui* advised his king on spiritual matters and conducted rituals to invoke spiritual help. *Kāhuna pule* performed invocations for assistance from the major spirits; some were of great length, and all required word-perfect recitation. *Kāhuna kilo hōkū* were experts in weather, seasonal changes, astronomy and navigation. *Kāhuna hoʻoūlu ʻai* were agricultural experts. *Kāhuna kālai* were carving experts. *Kāhuna kālai waʻa* were the master canoe builders. The *kahuna lāʻau lapaʻau* was a medical practitioner. There were also such specialists as *kāhuna hui*, who performed mortuary ceremonies for the deification of a king; *kāhuna kilokilo*, who observed the skies for omens, and *kāhuna kaula*, regarded as prophets.

The term *kahuna* (plural, *kāhuna*), derives from *kahu* (caretaker). Custodians of esoteric knowledge kept secret in order to preserve its *mana*, they no doubt also knew, as do leaders of modern trade and professional organizations, that the control of knowledge by restricting entry to the group (publicly justified today as a way of maintaining high standards) preserves the group's status and a favorable demand/supply ratio. Then, as now, knowledge was power—a manifestation of *mana* easily lost if not kept private to those deemed worthy of it.

Of several types of temples (*heiau*) the *luakini* was the most elaborate and largest. Dedicated to Kū as patron of politics and warfare, these were the *heiau* of the ruling chiefs. Gifts of food were regularly offered to propitiate Kū at the *luakini* altar, for it was believed that a spirit that was not fed would drift away. When deemed necessary, the gift of a man's life was made ("sacrifice" is the conventional term, but "gift" is descriptively more accurate). The act of killing was not part of the ritual—an enemy slain in battle, a criminal or slave knocked on the head and carried to the temple would do nicely—but it had to be a healthy man, never a woman, child, or a man with a deformity or wasted by age. As stated earlier, only the king could order it.

Waihau were *heiau* at which humans were not offered. Of these, the *māpele* were agricultural shrines to Lono, spiritual source of fertility, abundance and peace. *Heiau ho'ōla* were for healing.

Pu'uhonua were sanctuaries where fugitives could find safety from those pursuing them. Little is known about the conditions and terms which governed them, but it's believed that after some penance or adjudicated reconciliation a fugitive could depart without fear. The best known is Pu'uhonua o Hōnaunau, the sanctuary at Hōnaunau Bay, within the Ahupua'a of Hōnaunau, in the South Kona district of Hawai'i Island, now partially restored and preserved as the Pu'uhonua o Hōnaunau National Park.

The power of the *kāhuna* largely ended when the Kingdom of Hawai'i officially abandoned the ancient religion in 1819. For the ruling chiefs to abandon the *mana/kapu* system that was the very foundation of their power must have been a wrenching decision; and, despite 40 years of contact with foreigners, this was entirely their own decision. Christian missionaries did not influence them, having not yet arrived.

HŌNAUNAU BAY   The restored walls and platforms of the sanctuary and the mortuary of ancient chiefs, features of the Pu'uhonua o Hōnaunau National Park.   *Collection of Robert and Sandra Kamigaki*

Polynesians saw Europeans not as superior beings, but as another people who had apparently been blessed with materials and technology as beneficiaries of a god more powerful than their own *akua*. Moreover, their *akua* seemed powerless to protect them from foreign diseases against which Westerners seemed to have greater protection. And for thirty years Hawaiian sailors had been crewing on foreign ships, returning home with tales of powerful nations, any of whom could gobble up the Kingdom of Hawai'i. Clearly, the protection of international recognition was necessary. To gain recognition the Kingdom must become accepted by the West, which meant that Hawai'i must become westernized as rapidly as possible. Logically, this would require acceptance of the European God as the original source of all Western *mana*.

Pressured by advisors, including his *kahuna nui*, Liholiho (Kameha-meha II) abolished the *kapu* system, symbolically announcing his edict by violating the *kapu* against men and women eating together. To reinforce the point, images in local *heiau* were ordered destroyed.

Chiefs and priests who disapproved of Liholiho's actions gathered forces, rallied behind his cousin, Kekuaokalani, and marched on the capitol, Kailua, in Kona. The government force met them in Keauhou, in what became the Battle of Kuamo'o.

Accustomed to fighting in close quarters with hand weapons, many combatants were now armed with muskets. The battle became one of bloody attrition in which both sides stood their ground and shot it out. The government force prevailed, and the ancient religion went out in a blaze of musket fire.

Missionaries arrived a few months later to discover that their most difficult challenge had been swept aside. They endured a probationary period, but acceptance was inevitable. In requests for more funding from New England, however, it would not do to make their work seem too easy, and to contrast themselves with their native predecessors they were wont to cast themselves in an aura of goodness and refer to the *kāhuna* as evil seers and sorcerers. Foreigners as well as later generations of native converts came to cast all *kāhuna* in the mold of the *kahuna 'anā'anā*, specialist in spells which could cause death simply because the intended victim believed it.

Without writing, *kāhuna* were the living libraries of the old culture, preserving knowledge in trained memories. Some feats of memory seem incredible today. The story of Kamapua'a required sixteen hours of word-perfect recitation. Some temple invocations, we are told, in which any mistake would break the power of the words, required two days to deliver. Early Christian missionaries were astonished to find among their converts some who could recite entire books from the Bible soon after learning to read. Knowledge kept in living memories and shared only among a select few is extremely fragile, which helps explain why so much has been lost. One epidemic of an introduced disease could wipe out the masters of a guild, and with them knowledge accumulated over millennia. Disenfranchised in 1819 and subsequently condemned by Christian missionaries as sorcerers and witch doctors, their veil of secrecy became their shroud.

The image of the *kahuna* has gone through another transformation in this century with highly speculative books about *kahuna* mysticism and magic. But by their own lights, within their perceptions of their world, I believe the *kāhuna* regarded themselves not as mystics but as intensely pragmatic practitioners.

A CEREMONY AT PU'UKOHOLĀ HEIAU (now a National Historic Site) *Collection of the National Park Service*

KA'AHUMANU IN 1794
Artist's Collection

THE POWER OF WORDS

Modern Culture, Economics, Representative Government—the world as we know it—could not exist without broad dissemination of information. The written word is the vehicle of power. But writing was not invented in Polynesia because the very idea of its result, the uncontrolled dissemination of knowledge, was incompatible with the belief that knowledge was sacred power, a manifestation of *mana* that must be guarded as sacrosanct to those worthy of it.

In old Hawai'i, words were believed to have *mana* of their own. It was said, "A word thrown as a spear may fly back and slay the speaker." An invocation delivered by a *kahuna pule* would invoke spiritual help, it was believed, only if the delivery was word perfect, for the power was in the words. Words transmit *mana* as knowledge. The spoken word can be confined to a select audience, but the *mana* of written words made widely available could be dissipated or misused.

This view changed when Hawaiian chiefs discovered literacy as the key to understanding and using the power of Western culture. Soon after missionaries arrived in 1820, they published a reader in Hawaiian. This caught the interest of the Queen Regent Ka'ahumanu, and though she resisted conversion to Christianity for several years, she learned to read in five days. Schools were set up throughout the kingdom, and the people ordered to attend. By 1824 some 2,000 students were learning to read. By 1828, 37,000 were literate, and by 1831, 52,000—two-fifths of the entire population had graduated. Reading and writing had become an exciting new adventure.

Examinations in reading and writing were given four times a year, and graduations became occasions of great festivity. By 1834, a majority of the population had become literate. With the continuous passage of students through the schools, the Kingdom of Hawaii soon achieved what may have been the highest literacy rate of any nation in the world at that time, one which supported numerous Hawaiian language newspapers and other periodicals.

RECIPROCITY

No WORD FOR TRADE OR MERCHANT SEEMS TO HAVE EXISTED in any Polynesian language. Exchange of goods and services was by a system of reciprocal gift exchange, complicated by a protocol that recognized differences in status between the parties. Gifts honored the recipient and brought honor to the giver. When Hawaiians worked, they produced impressively, but when their needs were met, they ceased working—a custom regarded as laziness by Europeans accustomed to a market economy. The idea that work must extend beyond need, producing surpluses that might be used to expand an enterprise, was foreign to Hawaiians, as was the concept of trade for profit. Stinginess was unforgivable; a person's worth was measured less by how much one could accumulate than by how much one could give. Today, the urge to share surpluses presents a dilemma to many Polynesians trying to survive within the market economy.

While working in Fiji, I learned that any gift to my house servant would be turned over to her husband upon her return home, unless accompanied by a note insisting that it be for her alone. The gift might be passed to a family elder, then offered to the village chief, who might keep it, give it to someone else, or return it with his compliments; but all gained honor by its passage, whether offering the gift or receiving it.

In the custom of reciprocity (*uku* in Hawaiian, *utu* in Maori) acceptance of a gift obliges the recipient to reciprocate, bringing dishonor if he does not. In Polynesian societies, exchanges of goods or services promoted prosperity for all. Gifting could be of a ceremonial nature (*ho'okupu*) such as a gift to a chief or to honor someone, but always carried the obligation to reciprocate. The "sacrifices" offered at the temples of chiefs or the family shrines of commoners are more accurately described as gifts made in hopes of receiving spiritual help.

On the negative side, reciprocity requires the return of any injury. An insult or blow given to a member of one's extended family is taken as a personal outrage by every individual in the family, and honor requires that it be returned. The attitude is still strong among some Polynesian groups. When a member of a Samoan extended family new to Honolulu is arrested, police have learned to explain their action to the suspect's elders without delay.

An insult to a ruling chief could bring his entire community into battle. In 1783 King Kiwala'ō of the Island of Hawai'i, worried by the growing political strength of his charismatic cousin, Kamehameha, decided to lure the upstart into battle and rid himself of the threat. Kamehameha received Kiwala'ō and his chiefs hospitably at Kealakekua Bay, in the district of Kona, and prepared the ceremonial 'awa drink himself. But when he offered the first cup to his king as befitting his guest's high status, Kiwala'ō passed it to a person of low rank. Thus the insult was passed. Kamehameha's war chief drew him away, and both sides prepared for battle. Kamehameha was trapped.

But at the height of the Battle of Moku'ōhai, Kiwala'ō was struck down by a sling stone. The ruling chief of Kona, Ke'eaumoku, though desperately wounded and bleeding from many dagger thrusts, crawled to the unconscious Kiwala'ō and cut his throat with a shark-toothed weapon. At the death of their leader, the King's forces lost heart and fled. With this victory, Kamehameha began his drive toward supreme rule; first as King of Hawai'i Island, then extending his conquests to bring all the islands under the rule of the Kingdom of Hawai'i.*

*The State of Hawai'i inherited its name from what began as the Kingdom of Hawai'i (the Island).

SEA BATTLE AT MOKU'ŌHAI   During the land battle, rival canoe fleets fought off shore. *Copyright © National Geographic Society*

MAKAHIKI

Harvest Festival and Time For Tax Gathering, Makahiki was the season of Lono, patron spirit of agriculture, fertility, peace and healing. Beginning in late October with the rising of the Pleiades in the evening sky, Makahiki marked the time each year when the invisible Lono returned to repossess the land as his wife, bringing seminal rains and renewing its fertility. To make way for Lono, the People relinquished their hold on the land. Until early February the king vacated his role as mediator between his subjects and the spirit Kū, patron of the works of men. Without Kū's patronage, no important project of work, warfare or politics could be done. Having usurped the land for eight months, men now released it back to Lono so that its fertility might be restored.

Each island had its version of Makahiki. On Hawai'i, the season was announced by flags flying from the temples. On the first night, fires were lighted along the coast around the island. The people dressed in their best clothing and went down to the sea, where they removed their clothing, and spent the night bathing and swimming, making love as they pleased, and conversing in good humor as they warmed themselves at beach fires. This was the *hi'uwai*, a purification in water as a rite of passage to another season, accompanied by erotic activity which may have been intended to arouse Lono to his husbandly duty. At the first light of dawn, those who bathed at Kealakekua Bay saw, set in the sand on the beach, a tall pole with a small image carved at its upper end. A cross piece was tied below the image from which were hung long banners of white *kapa* (bark-cloth), feather pennants, ferns and imitation birds. This was the standard of Lono, the *akua loa*. For four days after the *hi'uwai*, no work of any kind was permitted.

A procession went around the island carrying the Lono standard. At the border of each district, it was set up and gifts of craftswork and food were brought to it. But just as men usurped the land from Lono, the gifts were taken by the chiefs, some to be kept as taxes, the rest to be distributed back to the people. In mock battle, those carrying the Lono standard were driven into the next district. Another standard, similar but with two banners, the *akua pā'ani* (spirit of games) was set up, and the people feasted and enjoyed sporting events and games.

Patron of these events was the spirit of a chief named Lono (not the great *akua* Lono) who ruled Hawai'i Island six generations before Kamehameha. He had sailed away, driven mad with remorse after killing his wife in a fit of jealousy. Recovering his sanity, he returned,

VISITORS FROM ANOTHER WORLD: Departing from a village on the Puna Coast of Hawai'i, the Makahiki procession of 1778-1779 pauses to watch the appearance of the Cook expedition.

regained his kingdom, and defeated an invasion from Maui. An ardent sports enthusiast, he instituted the Makahiki games, and after death was remembered as Lono-i-ka-makahiki (Lono of the Makahiki).

At the close of Makahiki the king, representing his people, ritually reappropriated the land from Lono in a mock battle. When the Makahiki image was returned to Kealakekua Bay, the king, with his retinue and warriors, landed on the beach from canoes. They were opposed by warriors with spears standing before the Lono image. As the king landed, preceded by one of his champions, one of the opposing party ran toward him holding two spears. One spear was hurled at the king, but was warded off by the king's champion; the second spear was not thrown, the man merely touching the king with it as he passed. A sham battle followed in which Lono's force was routed, and the king reasserted his dominion over the land. Once again, Men had usurped the land from Lono so that they might make a living from it. The *luakini*, state temples, were refurbished, reconsecrated to Kū and reopened.

WARRIOR CHIEFS

A council of chiefs discusses tactics before leading their commoners into battle. In the foreground, the man at left holds a weapon inset with shark teeth (*lei o mano*). Around his waist is a belly protector of strong matting decorated with feathers. His companion holds a throwing spear (*ihe*) and a stone headed club (*newa*). Throwing spears, long lances (*pololū*) and wooden daggers (*pahoa*) are seen among the men in the background.

As Captain Cook's men learned from personal experience, the feathered capes and helmets were "battle apparel." The cape might be worn over the shoulders, but in battle it was pulled around the left side of the body and held forward with the left hand to snag a thrust from a dagger or the point of a thrown spear. In this position the right arm was exposed and free to wield a weapon. Feathers were black, white, red, yellow, green and the long rust-red and black feathers of the fighting cock. These were tied over a light netting of cord in a great variety of designs. In battle, the brilliant capes helped warriors identify and rally to their chiefs. Helmets made of strong, light weight basketry protected the head from the impact of stones shot from slings.

Hawaiian tattoo designs were generally not as bold as those of the South Pacific. At their first glimpse of Polynesians, some early Europeans in the Pacific mistook Polynesian tattooing for tight-fitting clothing. Sailors who admired the art returned to Europe sporting Polynesian tattoos. "Tattoo" comes from the Tahitian *tātau* (Hawaiian *kākau*).

Collection of The Four Seasons Resort, Hualalai

WARFARE

THE HAWAIIAN INVENTION OF SURFING HAS BEEN CALLED "THE sport of kings," but in the shark-infested waters of ancient Hawaiian politics—well described in S.M. Kamakau's *Ruling Chiefs of Hawaii*—the supreme sport of kings was warfare. Political influence could be expanded by marriages and alliances, but for status-hungry chiefs, nothing relieved boredom like a decisive military campaign.

Kū, in his manifestation as Kūkā'ilimoku, was the patron spirit of warfare; his aid was sought at the *luakini heiau*. Before a battle, advice was sought from advisors, including *kāhuna* who read portents in such

natural phenomena as the shapes of clouds.

Meeting on a field of battle, champions of both forces stepped forward, shouting challenges. Legends tell of some disputes settled by duels between champions. At the last moment a battle might be avoided and the course changed to tearful reconciliation if a leading chief responded to a plea from a beloved relative on the other side.

We may picture a battle opening with volleys of sling stones, followed at closer range by thrown spears. If a stone thrown from the hand of a Polynesian was a deadly weapon, as some early European visitors discovered, the Hawaiian sling stone, shaped and polished from heavy basalt, could be delivered from a sling with force approaching that of a musket ball. Throwing spears, javelins six to eight feet long were shaped from *kauila*—a very hard wood so heavy it sinks in water.

Front and center at the moment of impact were warriors in close formation similar to the Greek phalanx, thrusting long lances. Daggers and clubs were used in close fighting. The usefulness of deceptive tactics and flanking maneuvers was exploited. Archery was practiced throughout Polynesia, shooting at targets and rats for sport, and, in one Hawaiian tale, at birds; but the bow was not a weapon of war, and no one knows why.

Women frequently accompanied their husbands into battle, sometimes fighting beside them. When threatened by invasion, women encumbered with children and the elderly sought places of refuge in forests and caves, or in *puʻuhonua* (sanctuaries).

Kamehameha was the first to bring all the islands under one rule, but not the first to try. Kalaunuiʻōhua, a 13th century chief, conquered all the islands except Kauaʻi, where his army was defeated on the beach. Many kings ruled with diplomacy and benevolence— Mailekūkahi of Oʻahu, Līloa of Hawaiʻi, and Līloa's son ʻUmi were especially noted for their wisdom and goodness; but ambition drove others to increase their power through conquest.

In times of peace, competitive games were substitutes for warfare. Boxing, fencing with staves, wrestling, and mock battles were sports useful in the training of warriors. At a jousting event, Kamehameha gave British Captain George Vancouver a demonstration of his skill. Stripping down to a loincloth, he stepped out before his men, and had six spears thrown at him simultaneously and with full force. He caught two, parried three and deflected one.

Such demonstrations were no doubt calculated to reassure people that their leader had the right stuff. Kahekili of Maui astonished his subjects by leaping into the sea from high cliffs. Speeding down a *hōlua* slide, risking death or injury if his narrow sled skidded over the edge of the steep ramp, a chief could demonstrate his *mana* during peacetime.

Facing page:
KAUHI'S LAST STAND
A 1738 battle for the rule of Maui
comes to an end at Kaʻanapali.
Collection of Amfac JMB Hawaiʻi

At right:
KAMEHAMEHA CATCHING SPEARS
Collection of William Donnelly

THE PETROGLYPH MAKER *Collection of Elizabeth Marshall*

COMMONERS

THE *MAKA'ĀINANA* WERE PLANTERS, ARTISANS, FISHERMEN, hunters and gatherers, performers, healers, sailors—the working people. Their status and rewards varied according to their skill and productivity. All able bodied men would follow their chiefs to war.

Commoners provided their chiefs with foods, craftswork, and labor. Chiefs were obligated to reciprocate with good governance and security. Unlike European serfs, *maka'āinana* afflicted by a cruel chief could move to another district, and there are a few accounts of rebellion. In general, there was a mutual respect between chiefs and commoners without which neither could succeed. Both classes accepted their differences of station as natural rather than culturally invented, and there seems to have been little yearning among commoners for social status higher than merited by their seniority within their extended families or earned by their own accomplishments.

The most frequent contacts between chiefs and commoners were the work planning conferences held daily by a lower chief, the *konohiki* (supervisor) of a particular land division, and the *haku*, leaders of guilds and spokesmen for extended families.

The 19th century historian S. M. Kamakau alluded to another point of contact when concluding biographies of ruling chiefs with the conventional remark, "he became an ancestor of chiefs and commoners." An affair between a generous chief and a *maka'āinana* woman was usually welcomed, for it could bring chiefly patronage to her entire family, especially if a child was produced.

Men did all heavy work, as well as the cooking. Women did light domestic tasks, cared for infants and young children, and devoted much time to making *kapa*, plaiting matting and twisting light cordage for fishlines and nets. Women helped with the making of gourd containers, and the evaporation of salt from seawater. They harvested some wild plants and seaweed, caught shellfish in the shallows along the beaches and reefs and fished for shrimp and small fish in freshwater streams. Their agricultural work was limited to tending beds of sweet potatoes. Upon the death of a husband, his nearest male relative would undertake the care of his widow, cooking her food and keeping her home in repair.

Boys remained with their mothers until their sixth year, when, with ceremony, they were permitted to eat with men and have their first taste of meat.

Wherever possible, work was done by sociable groups. Children learned by observing and working with their elders. The more arduous the task, the greater the number who would assemble for it. Projects involving great labor were often turned into festive occasions.

UNTOUCHABLES

As in some other Polynesian societies there was a small class of hapless slaves (*kauwā*) about whom very little is known. Believed to have no *mana*, they lived apart from the rest of society to avoid contact that might rob others of *mana*. They may have been men and women taken as prisoners of war or their descendants, for to be taken as a prisoner of war was the worst possible disgrace, causing the loss of all *mana* as well as rejection by their ancestral spirits. If caught trying to escape, anyone could put them to death. Human sacrifices, we are told, were sometimes taken from the *kauwā* men, those not feeble with age or deformed, and they were strangely resigned to their fate.

The *kauwā* disappeared early in the 19th century. In the turmoil of the first major epidemics and the mobility of the population after the abandonment of the *kapu* system and the acceptance of new ways, they may have moved to places where they were not known and quietly merged with the *maka'āinana*.

POUNDING POI FROM COOKED TARO ROOT

FOOD

THE THING MOST DEVOID OF SACREDNESS IN POLYNESIA WAS COOKED food. The pleasures of eating aside, *mana* was a potentially dangerous force not to be ingested. Because the conversion of flesh into food removed *mana*, cannibalism was practised in some South Pacific societies as the ultimate insult to a defeated warrior. This took a wry turn in Hawai'i, where a chief might have whimsical effigies of his enemies derisively carved in servile postures as supports for food platters.

Men and women took their meals separately to preserve the distinction between male and female *mana*, one which could be blurred by both sexes handling the same food. Some foods were forbidden to women, such as pork, certain kinds of fish and most types of bananas.

Most food was cooked in *imu*, earth ovens constructed by lining pits with stones. Men did the work, cooking the food for their women in separate *imu*. The method is a combination of roasting and steaming called *kālua*. A fire is built, and when the stones are glowing hot, the embers are removed and the foodstuffs, wrapped in wetted *tī*, ginger or banana leaves, are put into the pit and covered with wet leaves, mats and a layer of earth. Water may be admitted through a bamboo tube to create steam. The intense heat from the stones cooks the food thoroughly. Food for several days may be cooked at once, removed as needed, and the cover replaced to keep the remainder warm.

Sweet potatoes, taro, breadfruit and other vegetables were cooked in the *imu*, as well as fish. Chickens, pigs and dogs (their flesh made palatable by a vegetarian diet) went into the *imu* with hot stones inserted in the abdominal cavities. Sea salt was the condiment. *'Inamona*, a favorite relish, was made of roasted, mashed *kukui* nutmeats and salt, sometimes mixed with seaweeds.

Food was an integral part of hospitality. One who did not offer food to a visitor, though it be his last morsel, felt deeply shamed. Chiefs gave great feasts to honor important visitors as well as to signify their own status. Anyone who has witnessed Hawaiians working together to prepare a "go-for-broke" *lū'au* for a hundred or more guests cannot fail to be impressed by the logistics and cooperation involved.

Cannibalism was not practiced in Hawai'i, and is mentioned here only because tour conductors have found that bad jokes about the post-mortem treatment of Captain Cook will get their visitors' full attention. After Cook's death, when communication was restored, the British requested the return of his body. Receiving a package containing pieces of the corpse, they were moved to ask the dreadful question. The response was one of such genuine horror that the British were convinced no cannibalism had occurred.

Cook had been given the mortuary treatment of a high chief, merited by his obvious position of command over men, ships and an awesome technology. *Mana*, it was believed, reposed in the major bones. The flesh and small bones, considered worthless, were dumped off shore—a chore the British unwittingly performed for the Hawaiians by their own custom of burial at sea. The valued bones were cleaned, sometimes encased in plaited reliquaries, and treasured for their *mana* as important relics—not unlike the treatment given the remains of Christian saints.

The Painting:

PHYSICIAN

Wearing a lei of shredded *ti* leaves, a *kahuna lā'au lapa'au* prepares an infusion of herbs, some of which will be ground up in the stone mortar near his knee. Many remedies were gathered from the sea to the mountain forests, and some were cultivated. Smoke curls up behind him from a small fire over which *noni* leaves are being charred for use in a preparation.

He holds a sprig of *pōpolo*, perhaps the most important of all medicinal plants. The juice of the leaves and the black, sweet berries was used in treatments for skin disorders,wounds, and digestive problems. In the bowl at lower right are fruit and leaves of *noni*, perhaps the second most important plant in healing. Leaves of *kukui*, in the basket at right, were used as a laxative or a purge. A small bowl (lower center) holds red salt (*pa'akai 'alaea*) evaporated from sea water steeped in red ocherous earth. On the platter, right to left, are yellow-blossomed *'ilima*, the seaweed *limu kala*, and the corms of *'ōlena* (tumeric). Behind the platter are stalks of *kō* (Polynesian sugar cane). At lower left is the ginger *'awapuhi*.

At left, a broken bone is being set. It is said that specialists in bone setting went through a lengthy apprenticeship from which they graduated only after breaking and successfully setting a bone in a member of their family. At right, a physician manipulates the body of a patient with varying pressures calculated to help him make his diagnosis.

Physicians observed rituals expressing respect toward Lono, patron spirit of healing, and strived to emulate their ancestral *'aumakua*, conducting their lives in a manner that would make them worthy of receiving *mana*.

Collection of The Four Seasons Resort, Hualalai

The Painting:

PLAITER OF MATTING

A master craftswoman plaits (*ulana*) a fine-weave *lauhala* mat (*lau* means leaf, *hala* is the pandanus tree). She is seated on a coarse mat, but as the fine mat is enlarged she will move forward over it. Her head *lei* is made of seed keys of the ripe *hala* fruit. Fine mats were sometimes plaited with intricate designs using strips of dyed *lauhala*, and were often of great size. Very fine mats were also made from *makaloa*, a native sedge. Baskets, as pictured at right, were plaited from *lauhala* as well as from the aerial rootlets of the *'ie'ie* plant.

Three women work behind her in the shade of a *kou* tree. At left, *hala* leaves are whitened by being passed through smoke over a smudge fire of chunks of *hala* wood. At upper left, children gather fallen leaves from a *hala* grove. At upper right a woman with a sharpened shell knife scrapes the leaves to smooth and clean them (knives of split bamboo were also used). Thorny edges are stripped off the leaves. At extreme right, a girl winds leaves into coils for storage until they are needed for plaiting, moistening the dried leaves and alternately rolling them first in one direction, then the other, to make them pliable. The leaves are split into strips of the desired width before plaiting.

In the distance a canoe puts to sea, powered by a sail of *lauhala* matting. Tightly plaited and fitted mats were lashed over canoe hulls in rough weather to keep out the sea. In places where fresh water springs and streams were scarce, mats conducted rain water to collect in gourds. Matting was also used to roof temporary shelters while traveling, and for clothing in cold or wet weather. Commoners frequently wore protective capes of strong matting into battle.

Collection of The Four Seasons Resort, Hualalai

THE ANCIENT LANDSCAPE

IMAGINE YOURSELF AS AN EARLY FOREIGN VISITOR APPROACHING an island in the Hawaiian archipelago, someone with the curiosity of John Ledyard with Cook's expedition or Archibald Menzies with Vancouver's. While the land is still a distant blur, you might notice canoes of fishermen well out to sea, or large double canoes of chiefs on interisland travel, moving swiftly under sail in favorable winds, or paddled by many hands against the wind.

THE COOK EXPEDITION ENTERING KEALAKEKUA BAY, JANUARY 1779

59

Arriving at a Hawaiian coastal community, you would be astonished to see young people riding wooden boards upon the fringing surf, a sport seen nowhere else. On shore, canoes are being launched to join those which have come out to escort your ship to its anchorage. Of the many people in canoes, those in the chiefly double canoes wear clothing of a barkcloth which far surpasses any you may have seen in the South Pacific in the variety and beauty of its patterns, colors and textures. Many persons swimming or on surf boards, all naked in the water, cluster about the ship as it comes to anchor.

You join a party rowing ashore in one of the ship's boats, passing children swimming in the shallows. Small children playing on the beach are naked, but those who have passed their sixth year are clothed like their elders—the boys wearing loincloths, the girls in simple skirts wrapped about the waist. Both men and women may wear an outer garment, a large square of *kapa* worn with the corners joined over the left shoulder, or over both shoulders in cool weather.

If you're with the Cook expedition, your comrades will describe the people of this place as "friendly, generous, hospitable, vigorous," and as "honest traders." During the troubles leading to Cook's death, some will view the chiefs as "acquisitive," the people "thievish" and "insolent." Young women who appear to be of the "lower classes" will seem eager to engage in sexual play, but you suspect their reasons may not be entirely the same as those of London prostitutes. As an 18th century European, you are surprised to find people who bathe and clean their teeth several times daily.

If you land at Kealakekua Bay, with Cook in 1779 or Vancouver in 1792, the presence of a large temple standing behind the beach commands your attention. On top of a rectangular platform of rocks fitted without mortar, ten or twelve feet high at the seaward end, a

An interpretation of Hikiau Heiau, the temple at Kealakekua Bay, based on 1779 descriptions.

fence of natural poles encloses the temple structures. A large thatched house and several smaller structures are within the seaward end of the enclosure; at the inland end is the "oracle tower," a tall framework covered with white barkcloth, wherein a priest—some say while in a trance—might speak out with the voice of a great spirit. Large carved wooden images stand here, facing the center of the platform; the central image, representing Kūnuiākea, identifies this temple as a *luakini*, dedicated to the spirit Kū as patron of the king. Here also is an altar, a structure of poles and shelving upon which ritual gifts to Kū are placed— vegetables, fish, baked dogs and pigs, and, in the most grave circumstances, the bodies of men.

You find the community is divided into three sections. Behind the beach and around a brackish pond lies the residential enclave of the priests, bounded by rock walls extending from the temple to the base of a high cliff. Below the cliff flows a spring of fresh water from which the ship's casks are replenished. Southward along the lava coast lies a populous village of commoners. The cliff borders the northern shore of the bay. On the western shore lies the village of the chiefs.

Most traffic across the bay as well as to other districts is by canoe. For land travel, a coastal footpath encircles the island. Markers of rockwork are constructed wherever this path crosses boundaries between land divisions, and no commoner will cross these without permission. Other paths keep within a land division, extending from the shoreline inland, affording commoners access to the environs of their entire

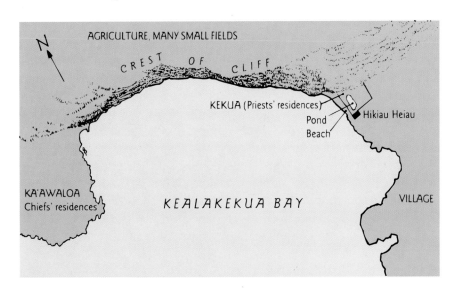

subdistrict from the sea to the mountains.

In the settlements you find each home to be a cluster of houses within a fenced compound, each structure serving a different purpose. Some have yards nearby, covered with small pebbles and walled in, where women are drying *kapa*. Most houses are not larger than 24 by 12 feet. Entrances are low, some with sliding wooden doors. In the common house, the family sleeps and socializes. There are separate eating houses for men and women. Some structures are built for storage, their floors elevated above the ground. Craftswork is done in the shade of flowering *kou*, or *milo* trees or under thatch-roofed shelters open to the breeze. Near the women's work area is a small hut for their confinement during their menstrual periods. Stalks of *tī* surround the houses, their presence warding off malevolent spirits, their broad leaves handy for a multitude of uses—food wrapping, disposable plates, bandages, crafts, or thatch to fix a leaky roof.

The homes are strongly built, typically set upon platforms of rocks fitted together without mortar and paved with pebbles or sand. Supporting posts are set firmly into this platform, and beams and rafters, carved to fit at the joints, are assembled with sennit lashings. This basic structure is covered with a framework of light poles over which thatching is attached—bundles of grasses, leaves of sugar cane or *tī*, or shingles of pandanus leaves. The ridges and gables of chiefs' houses or temple structures are often dressed with a thatching of ferns.

The flooring within is a thick cushioning of coarse mats covered by finely woven mats. Freshly cut grass spread under the top mats adds softness and fragrance. In the finest homes a sheathing of layers peeled from banana stalks might be applied to the interior walls, drying to a silky smoothness. Lounging and sleeping are done on platforms slightly elevated above the floor. The beds are cushions made of many layers of soft mats. Bedcovers and blankets are of soft *kapa*. Furnishings are wooden bowls, pounding boards and platters; containers and water bottles made from gourds, some encased in basketry and hanging in netting from wooden racks; baskets of various shapes and sizes; such utensils as coconut shell cups, knives shaped from stone flakes or split from lengths of bamboo, scrapers, peelers and cutters made by grinding sea shells to sharp edges, and mirrors of flat, polished stone, the surfaces wetted to enhance reflection.

In the village of chiefs on the western shore of the bay you find houses somewhat larger and more refined in construction. Intricate sennit lashings are decorative as well as functional. The compound of a

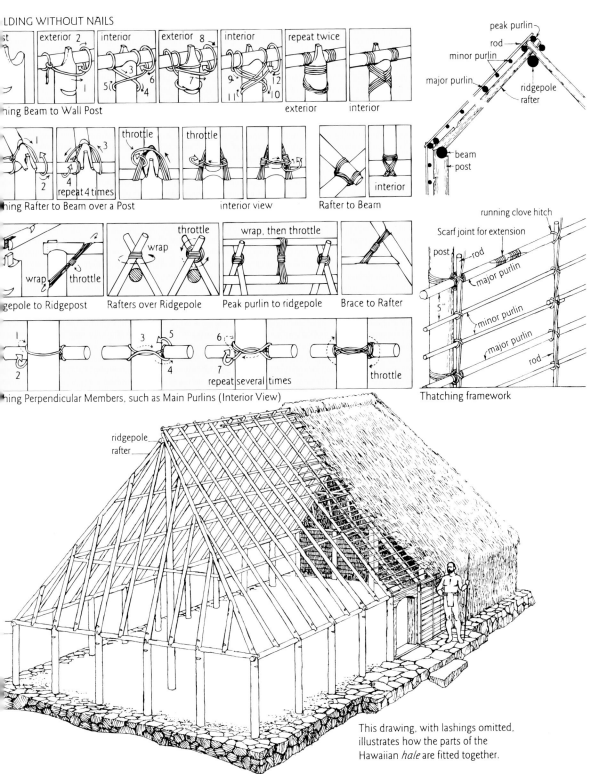

This drawing, with lashings omitted, illustrates how the parts of the Hawaiian *hale* are fitted together.

Making fire with the fire plough

paramount chief would contain a guard house, and possibly a shrine for the performance of rituals that do not require temple ceremony. You may see a man or boy making fire by the fire plow method, vigorously rubbing the end of a hardwood stick along a groove in a block of soft wood until friction ignites the wood dust accumulating at the end of the groove. A metaphor for sexual union, the work of making fire is restricted to men. Smoke or wisps of steam issuing from under crude shelters betray the presence of the family's earth ovens (*imu*), one for the men and another for the women.

In a corner of each men's dining house stands a little shrine to the family's ancestral spirits, perhaps a carved wooden figure or a naturally shaped stone. Before each meal, the leading elder places a little food at the shrine and offers a prayer of respect. The presence of spirits that are not fed cannot be invoked, for they have departed— leaping from the western-most point of each island, flying to an ancestral homeland in the west.

Along the seashore you may see salt obtained by evaporation of seawater. You pass through groves of coconut, one of the most useful of trees. Its nuts yield a refreshing drink, nutmeat, and oil. If left to sprout, the interior of the ripe nut fills with a white ball, crisp and deliciously sweet. The nut shells may be made into handsome cups, or burned for a warming small fire within a sleeping house, producing little smoke. Fiber from the husk is made into sennit cordage. The fronds may be used for thatching and basketry, and the trunk for wood—the base of the trunk for drums.

Groves of *milo* and *kou* trees also flourish along the shore, their wood favored for bowls and other carvings. At a work shelter you pause to watch a carver hollowing out a round bowl. Taking a tool resembling a bow compass—a curved flexible stick with a shark's tooth point at each end, the points connected by a taut cord—he adjusts the cord for the desired radius and scribes a circular cut in the wood. After excavating the interior of the circle with a basalt adze and chisel, he repeats the process, each time deepening the interior of the bowl.

In thatched canoe shelters, where only men may enter, new canoes are being completed and others repaired. The work, although done without metal tools, compares favorably with the cabinetry of Europe. Here, men too old for hard work sit in breezy shade, gossiping; some make or mend nets from a fine white cord superior in strength to anything you have seen; others roll coconut husk fibers against their thighs to produce a twisted twine, then braid it into the golden sennit that will be used wherever things need to be fastened.

Agriculture is intensive wherever there is topsoil. Even in areas of lava, gourds and sweet potatoes are grown within rock-walled enclosures where plant wastes have been composted.

As you move inland the land rises for several miles through scattered households among groves of bananas and many small fields of sweet potatoes and taro of the dry land varieties. Each field is bordered by rock walls, and along the walls are tall, feathery fringes of sugar cane. Pigs are kept in rock-walled pens, and chickens forage freely. Climbing higher, you come to breadfruit trees of such size, standing in groves so vast, that John Ledyard was moved to write, *"...behold now these breadfruit plains thine eye cannot discern their limits, and the trees are like the cedars of Lebanon in their number and in stature..."*

Above the breadfruit forests are more rock-walled fields of sweet potato and taro, wetted by afternoon showers. Higher, the land is thickly covered with ferns, some as large as trees. Then the ascent leads into the native forest dominated by tall *'ōhi'a* trees.

Small parties are gathering the aerial rootlets of *'ie'ie* for plaiting into strong basketry, or fragrant, leafy *maile* vines for *lei* making, or wild plants for medicines. Climbing

Following pages: KAANAPALI IN THE ANCIENT TIME
Collection of Amfac JMB Hawai'i

higher, you come upon a bird-catcher gathering feathers for a chief's cloak or helmet, or for a *lei* to adorn a lady's head. Trained in observing bird behavior and the techniques of snaring them in nets, he is also adept at imitating their calls, attracting them to land on poles tied to the branches of trees as inviting perches, and smeared with sticky gums. Some birds are killed for their feathers; others are plucked of their most colorful feathers and released to grow new ones.

Higher still, at perhaps two thousand feet elevation, the *koa* and *'iliahi* (sandalwood) forest begins. Here you may come upon a canoe-making party felling a giant *koa* or dubbing it out and roughly shaping it before hauling it down toward the shore.

As your altitude increases, so does the resistance of your guides. Here is more rain, and if you camp overnight you will be chilled by cold air flooding down from the summit of the great mountain they call Mauna

A TREE FOR A NEW CANOE
Collection of Walsh Hanley

Loa. Deep fissures in the lava, concealed by lush fern undergrowth, make each step hazardous, and you prudently turn back.

If your expedition lands on the windward sides of the islands, or wherever rainfall feeds streams of fresh water, you will find countless paddies of wetland *taro* growing in flooded terraces, each terrace raised by rock walls or earthen dams above the one below it. Water diverted from streams is channeled to the uppermost terrace, and descends from one terrace to another.

T HE POPULATION OF THE HAWAIIAN ISLANDS WAS ESTIMATED by James King, with the Cook expedition, as 400,000. But King saw only coastal settlements, and formed an opinion—disproved by later visitors—that the interiors held no settlements. A recent multi-disciplinary study has found this estimate much too low. Except for a brief stop at Waimea, Oahu, the Cook expedition landed only on the leeward sides of the islands. The windward sides, receiving more rainfall, sustained greater agricultural production and no doubt a larger population. Extensive remains of home sites, sweet potato enclosures and taro terraces irrigated by ancient watercourses on lands where these have not been erased by modern uses support a minimum estimate of 800,000 at that time—a population reduced to 40,000 a century later by the introduction of tuberculosis (which plagued Cook's officers), venereal disease (which plagued his men), and a host of other diseases devastating to a people who had no previous contact with them.

Wailing for the Dead

BUILDER

Carrying a coil of braided coconut fiber sennit (*'aha*), a master builder lashes the end rafter of a house to its supporting post and the lower roof beam.

Depicted clockwise from the rock wall builder at lower left, a man hands a shingle of thatch—made of pandanus leaves (*lauhala*) sewn over a light rod—to a worker lashing thatch to a rafter. Leaves of sugar cane, *tī* and bundles of *pili* grass were also used for thatching. Another worker completes the rafter lashings.

The building of walls and platforms of rocks fitted together and "dry-stacked" without mortar is a tradition alive and well today. Those who try it for the first time come away with great respect for the skill involved, not to mention bruised fingers. Masters of the art seem to know by intuition as well as experience how a particular rock will lock into place with others. Some may speak softly to a rock as they turn it in their hands, inspecting its shape, then dropping it into place. One worker explains, "The rock sort of tells me how it wants to be set."

Another, when asked what he does with the bad rocks, replied, "I don't know; I've never seen a bad rock."

A completed house (*hale*) is depicted at upper right, neatly trimmed with ferns at the ridge and gables, and set upon a rockwork platform (*kahua* or *paepae*) paved with pebbles or sand. "T" shaped racks from which storage gourds were hung stood beside the doorway. *Tī* plants were customarily planted near a house—the leaves had many domestic uses. At lower elevations the *kou* tree with the orange blossoms (at upper right) was favored for shade planting around homes.

At the opening of a new house the *piko* (umbilical cord, symbolized by a section of thatch left hanging over the doorway) was cut by the master house builder. Holding a board behind the *piko*, he cut it with an adze as he recited the appropriate invocation to ancestral spirits

Collection of The Four Seasons Resort, Hualalai

The Painting:

FISHERMAN

He wears a *ti* leaf rain cape and holds a yellow fin tuna (*ʻahi*). A favorite pearl shell lure with a bone hook is carried around his neck.

In the background, the presence of birds betrays a surface-feeding school of skipjack tuna (*aku*). Fishermen sail through the school, chumming the water and hauling in *aku* that have struck their lures.

At lower left, a man hunts the shallows with a spear of hardwood, lighting his way with a candlenut (*kukui*) torch. The oily dried nutmeats were strung on bamboo skewers to make candles, and a handful of these, stuffed into a section of bamboo and ignited, gave a bright light.

At lower right, men net a catch of silver perch (*āholehole*), a great delicacy.

Collection of The Four Seasons Resort, Hualalai

FISHING

THE MULTITUDE OF HAWAIIAN TERMS FOR FISH SPECIES, CLOUDS, winds, sea states, currents, sea birds, seasonal changes, and other natural phenomena, is evidence of their intimacy with the sea. Some fish had several names, each distinguishing a different growth phase. Hunting and harvesting from abundant reefs to the open sea, fishermen (*lawaiʻa*) developed a vast body of knowledge about their quarry.

They arose before dawn, assembling their gear and canoes quietly, and woe to anyone who interrupted their preparations. Were someone to ask, "Where are you going?" the expedition might be canceled on the chance that troublesome spirits may have been alerted. The master fisherman offered the first fish caught to his *kūʻula*—a special stone, either carved or natural, representing Kū in his manifestation as the patron spirit of fishermen. At fishing shrines (*koʻa*), often circular mounds of coral or rock, ceremonies were conducted to cause fish to increase.

In shoreline shallows and freshwater streams women and children caught small fish in traps and nets. In quiet pools boys learned to catch fish by hand, a skill that apparently must be acquired early in life or not at all—adults cannot seem to get the hang of it.

Conservation practices were observed in fishing, as well as in hunting and the gathering of wild plants, possibly a lesson learned from the disappearance of the large flightless birds early settlers had hunted to extinction. Fishing of *aku* (skipjack tuna) and *kawakawa* (bonito) was permitted during the first six months of the year, but *ʻōpelu* (mackerel) was *kapu*. *ʻŌpelu* could be taken in the last six months, but not *aku* and *kawakawa*. Protective *kapu* were placed on certain other fish during their spawning season.

There were many ways of netting. Schools of fish were encircled by canoes towing the ends of seine nets. Hundreds of feet long, the nets were suspended from wood floats and weighted along the bottom by stone sinkers. As the circle of netting was closed, the fish were driven into a large bag net in the center.

In shallow water, the ends of a seine net, also fitted with floats and sinkers, were fastened to poles held upright by a man at each end. Other men spread out and made their way back toward the net, beating the water. As the fish were driven to the net, the ends were drawn together to enclose them.

Dip nets were square pieces of netting attached at the corners to the ends of two flexible sticks, which arched diagonally over the net and were suspended from a line attached where the sticks crossed. Sinkers were tied to the ends of the sticks. The fisherman chewed oily *kukui* nuts which he spat over the surface of the water to improve visibility. Fish were attracted over the net by bait or by a hooked fish played as a decoy. As the net was pulled up, the weight of the sinkers brought the ends of the flexible sticks closer together, forming a bag in

NIGHT FISHING IN OLD HAWAI'I: As the sky darkened, men prowled the shallow waters of lagoons with torches and spears. "Candles" were made by stringing dried nutmeats of the oily *kukui* nut on thin skewers of bamboo. The top nut was ignited, and as it burned out it ignited the nut below it. For a fishing torch, clusters of these candles were lighted and carried in a bamboo tube. Spears were six to seven feet long, of hard wood with tips tapered to a point and fire-hardened. *Collection of Lewis and Darra Strauss*

THE DIP NET
(described in the text on the opposite page)

MAKING A FISH TRAP

the net and capturing the fish. Bait sticks of *kauila*, a wood heavier than water, were sometimes used, covered with the baked meat of *kukui* nuts and coconuts, all held together by a wrapping of the fibrous cloth-like material found at the base of coconut fronds.

All fine cordage, including that used in netting and fishing line, was twisted from fibers of the inner bark of the *olonā* shrub.

Fishtraps of many shapes and sizes were made from the aerial roots of the *ʻieʻie*, a climbing plant found at altitudes above 1,500 feet. Each trap had a funnel projecting downward into its interior through which fish would be lured by bait in the trap, and a bottom opening with a flap. While in use, this flap was kept closed by a flat stone which also served as an anchor.

Hawaiians developed a unique system for raising mullet (*ʻanae*), milkfish (*awa*), and flagtail (*āholehole*). Ponds (*loko*) were connected by channels to the sea, or formed by enclosing shallow coves with seawalls. A weir, a grate of narrow poles (*mākāhā*), was installed at the opening between the pond and the sea. Young fish hatched at sea, attracted by freshwater springs or algae, entered the ponds through the grate. Grazing and fattening on algae within the pond, they became too large to escape through the grating, and could be netted as needed for chiefly fare.

The sanctity of fishponds was believed to be guarded by *moʻo*, water spirits who might appear as lizards or turtles, sometimes sighted as a girl or woman sitting beside a pond and combing her hair. As an act of respect, a custodian of a fishpond washed himself before entering its water.

In bays and lagoons an entire community frequently joined in a *hukilau*. A line of people moved through the water carrying a long rope to which *ti* leaves were fastened, beating the water and making a great commotion, driving the fish ahead of them into a netted enclosure. The net was hauled ashore and the fish distributed to all.

THE SHARK STRIKES AT SUNDOWN

Rising to the scent of a basket of meat, a shark is lured into a weighted noose slung between the hulls of a double canoe. The line is payed out as the shark continues moving forward; then the line is jerked taut and the canoe taken on a wild ride. After the shark tires, another noose is slipped over its tail and the fish pulled backward until it drowns.

SWIMMERS AND SURFERS today seem not to have learned the rules our Hawaiian elders enforced when this writer was a boy: Don't swim at sunset or sunrise—sharks feed close to the surface when the sun is low in the sky or on cloudy days. Stay out of murky water, such as where streams enter the sea—sharks gather there. And don't swim while the *wiliwili* tree is in blossom. This last rule is ancient and no reason is given for it, but a recent compilation of recorded shark attacks in Hawaiian waters shows that twice as many occured in April (when the *wiliwili* blooms) as in any other month.

Driving fish at a *hukilau* (*described on opposite page*)

HŌNAUNAU BAY, SUNSET
Sails down, fishing canoes return from the sea. In the background is the ancient sanctuary, *Puʻuhonua o Hōnaunau*, now a National Park.

FISHHOOKS were crafted in a wide variety of shapes and sizes. from bone, pearl shell and wood.

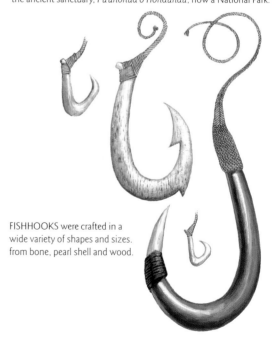

OCTOPUS LURES were crafted from a grooved and shaped stone, a cowrie shell, a bone hook, and a skirt of strips of *tī* leaves or *kapa*, all assembled to a wood shaft with cordage of *olonā* fiber . The stone represents the husband to the pretty cowry shell. When joined, they dance in the ocean. The octopus watches and cannot resist the cowry, its favorite food. As the stone touches the bottom, the shell is exposed above it and the hook is hidden by the skirt. When the octopus seizes the cowry shell, it may be hooked.

NET SHUTTLE; BAIT STICK; GOURD CONTAINER FOR LINE OR HOOKS

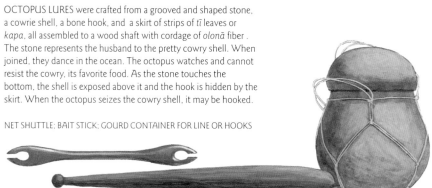

The Painting:

PLANTER

Standing among his *taro* plants, a planter (*mahi'ai*) holds a hardwood digging stick (*'ō'ō*) and a stalk of *taro.** "Wetland" *taro* was grown in shallow, earthen walled ponds (*lo'i*) irrigated by water diverted from streams, the water circulating through each pond, then spilling to the pond below it. "Dryland" *taro* was grown in rainy uplands or wherever water could be carried to the plants.

Behind the planter, a man carries bananas and breadfruit (*'ulu*) suspended from a carrying pole. At left, gourds (*ipu*) are grown in an enclosure of rock wall filled with humus—decomposed grass cuttings and other plant waste. A trellis of poles is laid over the enclosure and the vines trained so the fruit will hang from the trellis. Large gourds may be supported by cushions of leaves. Gourds can be decoratively shaped as they grow by tying them with cords, creating patterns where the cords restrict growth. Wherever there was no topsoil, planting was done in humus-filled enclosures. Breadfruit (upper left) flourished in large groves as a labor-free source of food, until cattle and goats, imported by Europeans, ate the sprouts of young trees.

Women did some light work, usually associated with the cultivation of sweet potatoes (*'uala*). At right, a girl harvests sweet potatoes from another rock-walled enclosure. Rising behind her is a stand of sugar cane (*kō*), a patch of banana (*mai'a*), and coconut palms (*niu*).

Collection of The Four Seasons Resort, Hualalai

*In the 19th century the Hawaiian language changed, *T* becoming *K* and *R* becoming *L*. The names of two plants, *taro* and *ti*, changed to *kalo* and *ki* in formally spoken Hawaiian. However, the ancient pronunciations (which have also been adopted by English speakers) remain in the widest use, and are used in this book.

PLANTING

Nowhere in Polynesia was the Cultivation Of Plants brought to a higher state of refinement than in Hawai'i. Evidence is in the fact that at least 85 named varieties of *taro* and 24 of sweet potato were developed by Hawaiian planters from those few brought by canoes from the South Pacific. Wherever land has not been reshaped for plantations, ranches, and other modern uses, archaeologists are still discovering terraces, irrigation ditches, aqueducts and homesites long concealed by overgrowth. In old Hawai'i, the numbers of planters far exceeded any other occupation.

By all accounts Hawaiian planters were deeply attached to their work and found it satisfying. Work was done by teams, seldom by individuals. When planting a prepared field, men sometimes moved forward in ranks as if in a dance, chanting, performing in unison the routine motions of opening the hole with their digging sticks, inserting the plant, closing the hole, and stepping forward to repeat the procedure.

Planting, cultivation, and harvesting conformed to traditions based upon a large body of knowledge of plants, soils, irrigation, seasonal cycles and weather. Planting was regulated according to phases of the moon; certain days of the lunar month were believed propitious for planting certain crops. Nor could an abundant harvest be expected without prayers and offerings to the great spirits, Kū, Lono, and Kāne. The men's work of agriculture was done under the patronage of Kū, but Lono's rains made soil fertile, and Kāne's sunlight invigorated growth.

Of all food plants *taro* was most valued, and much lore is associated with it; but the sweet potato, widely planted over vast inland slopes and plateaus, may have been the largest single crop.

POLYNESIAN HERITAGE PLANTS

Essential to their culture, these plants were brought to Hawai'i by ancient voyagers from the South Pacific. Of mostly Asian origin, many new varieties were developed by Hawaiian planters.

'AWA Piperaceae
Piper methysticum (kava)
Thought to be indigenous to Eastern Malaysia and widely spread by early canoe voyagers, the root was chewed or pounded and mixed with water as a ceremonial and social drink, inducing a feeling of well-being. Excessive use causes numbing and paralysis, primarily of the leg muscles. *'Awa* was also used medicinally, to relieve pain, and as a hypnotic.

'AWAPUHI Zingiberaceae
Zingiber zerumbet
(shampoo ginger)
Juices from the flowers were used by early Hawaiians as shampoo. The powdered root was used for scenting *kapa* (barkcloth), and the roots and leaves had medicinal uses. The plant is one of a genus of 80 to 100 species spread from Tropical Asia through the tropical Pacific islands.

HAU Malvaceae
Hibiscus tiliaceus
The strong but light-weight wood of this tree was used for canoe spars, outrigger floats and connective booms, and net floats. Rope was sometimes made from the bark. The flowers and bark were used in medicines. *Hau* is one of 200 species of the hibiscus family, spread world wide in tropical and subtropical regions.

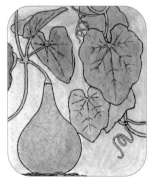

IPU Cucurbitaceae
Lagenaria siceraria (bottle gourd)
A Polynesian introduction that never naturalized in the wild, gourds were used in many shapes and sizes for containers and musical instruments. Some were huge and encased in protective basketwork. Others were elaborately decorated. The huge *ipu nui* developed only in Hawai'i have disappeared, possibly by mutation caused by the introduction of melons or by the arrival of an insect.

KALO, or TARO Araceae
Colocasia esculenta (taro)
Cultivated for its edible tubers, stems and leaves, it was the most important plant to Hawaiians. 80 cultivars are known in Hawai'i, where diversity reached a higher level than anywhere else (the language names 300 varieties). Used mostly for *poi* (cooked and pounded with water), it also had religious and medicinal uses, was used as bait in net fishing, as a glue, and in a dye for *kapa*.

KAMANI Clusiaceae
Calophyllum inophyllum
A large tree native to Eastern Africa, India, Southeast Asia, and Australia, it was an important medicinal plant. The wood was carved into containers, the flowers and sap were used for perfuming *kapa*, and oil processed from the dried nuts was sometimes used for lamp oil.

KŌ Poaceae
Saccharum officinarum
(sugar cane)
A genus of over 30 species of grass found throughout the tropics, this one is probably of Asian origin. Hawaiians grew 40 varieties. The stalks were chewed for their sweetness, the leaves were used for thatching, and the plant was also a source of fiber for craftswork.

KOU Boraginaceae
Cordia subcordata
Kou was a favored shade tree, loved for its orange blossoms that were sewn into *lei*. The wood was used in fine carving, and favored for food containers because it does not impart a flavor to the food (as does *koa*). Seeds were eaten and the leaves used to color fishing nets. Of Southeast Asian origin, *kou* is one of 250 species from the world's tropic and subtropic regions.

KUKUI Euphorbiaceae
Aleurites moluccana (candlenut)
A large tree. The bark was used in dyes. The wood was used for small canoes and carvings. Dried oily nutmeats, strung on skewers, were burned like candles for lighting in homes and for torch fishing. The oil was used for polish, in paints and as body oil. The nutmeats were used in medicines, as a laxative, and roasted and ground as an ingredient in a relish.

MAI'A Musaceae
Musa paradisiaca (banana)
About 20 of an estimated 70 varieties remain in cultivation. Three main groups are: *maoli*, which have long fruit; *iholena* with moderate fruit and orange flesh, and *popoulu* with shorter, thicker fruit. Almost all were cooked for food and offerings. The leaves were used to cover the *lele* (altar). Leaves and stalks were used as wrappings in preparing the *imu* (earth oven).

NIU Aracaceae
Cocos nucifera (coconut)
The Pacific tree of life. Two forms came with early Polynesians—one yellow-fruited, which was used by all, and one dark green-fruited, for ceremonial and medicinal uses. The fronds provided thatch and material for basketry, and the midribs of leaflets were bunched as brooms. The nuts provided meat, drink, oil and containers; the husk fibers were made into cordage; the wood was used in construction and for drums.

MILO Malvaceae
Thespesia populnea

A pan-tropical small to medium tree native to the Old World, *milo* produces a fine carving wood of beautiful color, favored for bowls and some sculptures. Like *kou* it was used for eating utensils as it did not impart a flavor to the food.

NONI Rubiaceae
Morinda citrifolia
(Indian Mulberry)

A shrub or small tree having large glossy leaves and fruit ranging from white to a ripe yellow. A tropical genus of mulberry native to Southeast Asia and Australia. In Polynesia, the fruit and leaves are used in many native medicines, and the roots were used in making a yellow *kapa* dye. It was also used in an insecticide.

'OHE Poaceae
Schizostachyum glaucifolium
(bamboo)

Not as plentiful as the more recent introductions. Its many uses included construction, the making of fine stencils for *kapa*, musical instruments such as the *pu ili* (split bamboo rattles), the nose flute (*ohe hano ihu*), and bamboo percussion pipes (*ohe keeke*). A genus of 25 species found in Asia, India, and the South Pacific.

'ŌHI'A 'AI Myrtaceae
Syzygium malaccense
(mountain apple)

Thought to have originated in Southeast Asia. The trunks were used for posts and rafters and some temple enclosures. The sweet fruit was eaten, and an infusion of the bark was used medicinally as well as in a dye for *kapa*.

'ŌLENA Zingiberaceae
Curcuma longa (tumeric)

Probably native to India, this herb was used as an important source of medicine and a yellow dye, and used in some religious practices.

PIA Taccaceae
Tacca leontopetaloides
(arrowroot)

No longer common in Hawai'i, its main use was as a fine starch. Its tubers were cooked and eaten in times of famine. Medicinally it was used in treatment for diarrhea and dysentery. *Pia* is native to the tropics from West Africa through Tropical Asia and Northern Australia. It is still an important plant in some Polynesian communities.

PŪHALA (or HALA) Pandanaceae
Pandanus tectorius (pandanus)
Plaited into mats, sails, and baskets, the leaves were also used for thatch and the root fibers for cordage. The fruit is made up of separate "keys" containing edible starch. Dried fibrous keys were used as brushes, and the colorful ripe keys for *lei* making. Four varieties are recognized by fruit color: *hala*, yellow; *hala 'ula*, orange; *hala lihilihi 'ula*, red; and *hala pia*, small, pale yellow keys.

TĪ (or KĪ) Agavaceae
Cordyline fruticosa
Planted near Hawaiian homes, *ti* was kept handy for thatch, food wrappings, sandals, rain capes, and bandages. It was also a charm against evil spirits. Stalks of *ti* served as flags of peace or truce. Physicians and priests wore the leaves around their necks. The large, sweet starchy roots were baked as a dessert. After Europeans arrived the roots were fermented and distilled into alcohol. Today, the leaves are also used for *hula* skirts.

'UALA Convolvulaceae
Ipomoea batatas (sweet potato)
Sweet potatoes ranked second to *taro* as the staple food. It may be the only Polynesian plant of American origin. Of 230 cultivars named, 14 are known to be naturalized. All but 24 can no longer be found. Stem tips, young leaves and tubers were eaten and various parts used medicinally. Vines were used as fodder for pigs as well as padding under mats. Cooked and mashed, the tubers were used as bait in net fishing.

UHI Dioscoreceae
Dioscorea alata (yam)
A genus of some 600 tropical and subtropical species of true yam, not to be confused with the variety of sweet potato labeled as the 'yams' found in groceries. Originally from Southeast Asia, the tubers were cooked and eaten when the preferred *taro* and sweet potatoes were in short supply. Early European ship captains sought yams as provisions which 'kept' longer than sweet potatoes.

ULU Moraceae
Artocarpus communis (breadfruit)
A large-leafed tree originating in tropical Asia and found throughout Oceania. The fruit was cooked as food, the light wood used for canoes, the bark for *kapa*, and the milky sap rendered in fire made a glue for caulking seams and cracks in canoemaking. The coarse male flower heads were used as a fine "sanding paper."

WAUKE Moraceae
Broussonetia papyrifera
(paper mulberry)
Native to China and probably Southeast Asia, it was cultivated by Pacific Islanders for its white inner bark from which the finest *kapa* (barkcloth) was made. *Wauke* fiber was also used in making a strong cordage.

Facing page, top: PLAITING SAIL MATTING
bottom: BRAIDING SENNIT

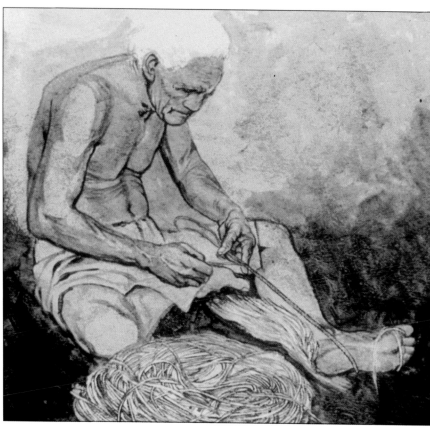

The Painting:

MAKER OF *KAPA*

Working with an engraved beater, the expert in the foreground embosses a water-mark pattern into a sheet of moist *kapa*, dyed yellow with *'ōlena* (tumeric). Her *kapa* wrap is colored a soft purple with a dye made by mixing lime (from burnt coral) with the juice of *'uki'uki* berries, and stamped in black with the sea urchin (*wana*) design. She wears a head lei of *'ilima* blossoms and a lei of polished *kukui* nuts.

At left, raw bark is given its first beating with a cylindrical beater (*hohoa*) upon a stone anvil (*kua*). A woman is stripping bark from a *wauke* (paper mulberry) sapling, as another flattens it by rolling. Two women lift a sheet of *kapa* from a dye bath. A girl at upper right prunes branching shoots from *wauke* saplings before their growth flaws the bark. Another scrapes strips of bark with a sharp shell.

At middle right, pigments are being ground in a stone mortar. Roots and bark of various plants were used in dyes. Bowls contain a lump of red earth and burnt coral. A large sheet of dyed *kapa* is being printed with geometric designs carved into stamps of bamboo. Black ink made from the soot of burnt *kukui* nuts, and red made from red earth, are applied to the printing sticks with brushes made from the dried keys of pandanus fruit.

Collection of the Four Seasons Hualalai Resort

Below: Magnified details of watermarking created with engraved beaters on damp *kapa* by artist Puanani Van Dorpe. *Left to right:* The traditional designs are abstractions of fish eyes, shark teeth, and ferns

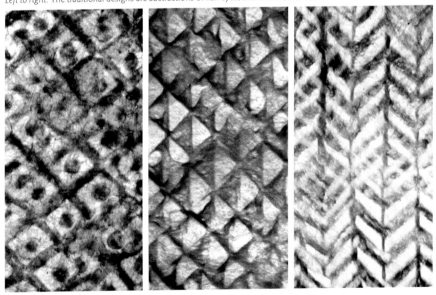

KAPA

Throughout Polynesia *TAPA* (barkcloth made from the soft inner bark of the paper mulberry and certain other trees) took the place of woven fabric. It is now called *kapa* in Hawai'i, where unique processes were developed which pushed the art to its highest refinement, both in the quality of the material and the variety and artistry of decoration. It was used for garments, sleeping coverings, and for wrapping precious objects. The finest was used as gifts symbolic of rank and prestige.

Hawaiian women worked under the patronage of the sister spirits Lauhuki and La'ahana to whom they offered prayers at a small shrine. The sound of *kapa* beating was heard throughout the day in Hawaiian communities. Women worked in congenial groups, and it's said that they could signal private messages to others in the sisterhood by the rhythms of their beating. Successive beatings of the bark over stone and wooden anvils, combined with complicated soaking and fermenting processes to soften it, produced wide strips. Larger sheets were made throughout Polynesia by overlapping these strips at the edges and beating them together; but Hawaiians went further—fermenting, mashing and felting the bark pulp to produce soft, paper-thin sheets that were truly seamless.

Kapa was often embossed in a final watermarking with beaters incised with intricate geometric designs. *Kapa* was dyed and pigmented in a wide variety of colors, and elaborate designs were often added by printing, stenciling or brushing. Some *kapa* was made by fastening several thin, delicate sheets together. Very thin sheets might also be layered together by beating, with the color and designs of one layer showing through the one above it. Bed sheets were sometimes made with sandalwood shavings between layers to add a pleasant fragrance.

The art of Hawaiian *kapa* declined after it was replaced by imported fabrics, and the specialized knowledge by which it was produced was largely forgotten. But in 1979, *kapa* artist Puanani Van Dorpe began gathering old accounts of processes and techniques, recorded long ago but never put to test. Patiently testing each account in controlled experiments, she has learned which ones are valid. She can now produce *kapa* identical to that made centuries ago, and her work is sought by art collectors. The *kapa* in this book are examples of her artistry.

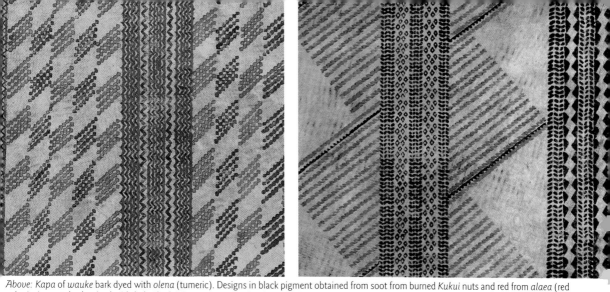

Above: Kapa of *wauke* bark dyed with *olena* (tumeric). Designs in black pigment obtained from soot from burned *Kukui* nuts and red from *alaea* (red ochre) pigment, both mixed with *kukui* bark juices, were applied with carved bamboo stamps. A rich variety of design was expressed with this palette.

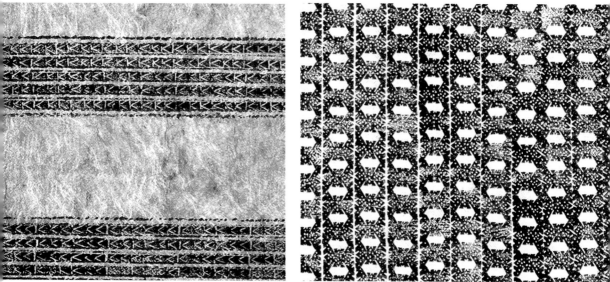

Above, left: Kapa from *ulu* (breadfruit) bark marked with bamboo stamps and dye-soaked cords. *Above, right:* Kapa from *akia* bark stamped with wood stamps in the flying bat design. *Below, left:* A multi-layered *kapa*, the black layer perforated with a shell auger, honors Lauhuki, patron spirit *kapa* makers. *Below right:* Kapa dyed with *akala* berries, and stamped with dye-soaked cordage and in the shark tooth design applied with wooden stamps.

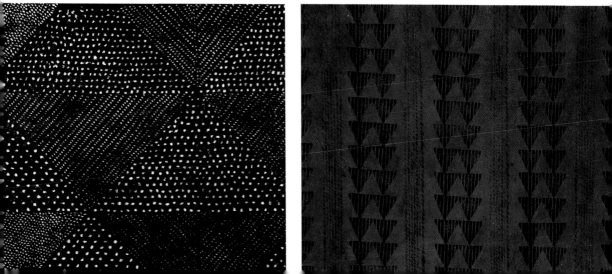

The Painting:

ADZE MAKER

The upper background of the painting depicts a man working the ancient quarry on the mountain Mauna Kea. The worker swings a large hammer stone between his legs against the edge of a basalt boulder core. If struck correctly, large flakes are produced of which some may be selected as adze blanks.

At upper left an adze (*ko'i*) is being shaped by a craftsman using a small hammer stone to remove flakes from both faces of a blank. This work was usually done at the quarry, after which the roughly shaped blanks were carried down the mountainside to the workplace of a master.

In the foreground, a master craftsman does the final flaking to produce the distinctively "shouldered" shape of the Eastern Polynesian adze. Each flake sets up further flaking by leaving what may be called a striking platform against which the next blow of the hammer stone may fall. As the size of the flakes becomes smaller, the overall shape of the adze becomes more refined.

After the final flaking, a craftsman (at left) grinds the adze against a wetted slab of fine-grained stone, using as grinding mediums pastes of various abrasives mixed with water, with more water added at intervals. An hour or two of grinding was required to produce flat faces that tapered to a sharp blade. Tools dulled by use were sharpened by further grinding.

The figure at right is lashing an adze to a haft carved from a section of a tree branch from which a thinner branch, the handle, has grown at an angle of approximately 70 degrees. The stone is set against a shock-absorbing cushion of bark cloth, and lashed up with braided sennit.

Collection of The Four Seasons Resort, Hualalai

TOOLS

In a World Without Metal, All Woodworking Was Done With tools of stone, shell, bone or the teeth of animals. The adze (*ko'i*) was the supreme implement, valued above all others.

The "shouldered" shape of the Eastern Polynesian adze is like no other in the world. No doubt it evolved because the shapes of adzes that proved most efficient to work with would be copied and refined. Efficient adzes expressed the *mana* of skilled adze makers, and were believed to accumulate *mana* through their use by expert craftsmen. While their owners slept, such tools might be "put to sleep" within shrines where it was believed they would be charged with spieritual *mana*. The deep respect for the adze was expressed in some Polynesian islands by fashioning special adzes as art objects for ceremonial rather than utilitarian purpose, with long blades superbly polished and mounted to ornate handles with decoratively intricate lashings.

Polynesian adzes were flaked from hard, dense basalt, and produced in many sizes to answer special needs. Chisels, knives, and drill bits were also fashioned from basalt flakes.

The adze is like an axe with the blade set at a right angle to the handle instead of parallel. The metal axe is so prevalent today that few

THE ADZE STROKE

people know what an adze is; but the adze is the best tool for shaping wood, and adzes are used by Pacific Islanders today, metal blades having replaced those of stone. The axe cuts quicker, but it's worthless for carving or canoe work; he who tries trimming a canoe log with it may find that one glancing blow can also trim off a leg.

The cutting edge of a stone tool necessarily has a bevel more obtuse than that of a metal blade, one that cuts less by slicing than by breaking the wood fibers under the force of a blow, leaving a subtly scalloped surface. Large adzes were used for rough work, the handles gripped in both hands with the thumbs lying along the handle. Smaller, lighter adzes were used for sculpting, held in one hand, often with the index finger extended along the handle to guide the stroke. Where sculptors use a large chisel or gouge today, requiring one hand to hold it and the other to swing a mallet, the workpiece must be secured by clamping to keep it from moving, and the carver must move around it or move the piece and re-clamp it. Such work can be done with a light adze using only one hand to make the stroke, leaving the other hand free to manipulate the workpiece. The carver does not change his position; his stroke remains constant and precise while the workpiece can be turned with the other hand. Only when woodwork became too fine for the smallest adze did Polynesians turn to chisels and scrapers.

Because stone edges dulled quickly, expert adzemen were assisted by helpers who removed dulled adze heads from their handles, sharpened their cutting edges on grinding stones, and re-lashed them.

Pounders, mortars, sling stones, stones used in bowling, and canoe anchors were shaped not by flaking but by "pecking," a method in which a workpiece of softer stone is struck repeatedly with a hammer stone to break up and remove the surface.

Very fine cutting, such as required to fashion a fishhook from a piece of shell, might be done by repeatedly engraving and deepening the cut with a tool pointed with a sharpened flake of the hardest basalt, a shark tooth or a rat incisor tooth.

OBJECTS SHAPED BY PECKING

SLING STONE

POI POUNDERS   CANOE ANCHOR OR CANOE BREAKER   KUKUI NUT LAMP   MORTER AND PESTLE

The Painting:

CANOE BUILDER

A master canoe designer (*kahuna kālai waʻa*) holds a pump drill and carries a small trimming adze in a sennit sling around his neck. At upper left, in the high, misty forest, a man cuts two grooves around the base of a *koa* tree, then breaks off the wood between them, repeating the procedure until the tree falls.

Kū, in his manifestation as Kū-pāʻaikeʻe, was the patron spirit of canoe-makers. It was believed that his wife, Lea, could appear before canoemakers as a little woodpecker, the *ʻelepaio*. If the bird alighted on a tree and pecked on the bark, it was taken as a sign that the wood was damaged by rot; but if the bird inspected the trunk and flew away without pecking, the wood was sound and could be taken. At the selected tree, offerings of fish and pork were made to Kū-pāʻaikeʻe. The new canoe would be named and vested with status not unlike that of a living person. As a great tree fell, the *kahuna kālai waʻa* shouted, "Today you are a tree; tomorrow you will become a man."

After a canoe was roughly shaped (at left), long ropes were made fast to it. For a canoe of great size an entire community might turn out, women shouting encouragement as men cleared the way and hauled it down to the canoe house at the shore, making an exciting event of heavy work. At the canoe *hālau* (upper right) the parts of the canoe received final shaping and finishing, and were assembled with braided sennit. Paddles, spars, bailers and other accessories were made ready. The man at right is smoothing the surface of a paddle with abrasive coral and lava rasps, working from coarse to fine. Men too old for heavy work sat in the canoe house, braiding miles of sennit (lower left).

A typical assembly of the hull, gunwale strakes, and crossbeams by lashings of sennit is depicted in the section view at right. Lashing methods varied; some were extremely intricate, done by the master builder in solitude lest others learn his technique; some were ornamented by using both black and red braided sennit.

Below is the classical form of Hawaiian double canoe (*waʻa kaulua*) as it had evolved by the time of European contact.

Collection of The Four Seasons Resort, Hualalai

CANOES

POLYNESIA BEGAN WITH THE VOYAGING CANOE. PROVEN SEAWORTHY upon Earth's largest ocean, it must rank as the finest product of any culture that knew no metals.

Among Pacific Islanders the canoe (Hawaiian *wa'a*, Maori *waka*) is the symbol of their mutuality. It lies at the heart of their culture, for all know that their very existence is owed to successful voyages in ancient canoes. The canoe reminds them of the courage, resourcefulness and skills of their ancestors—qualities worthy of emulation today, and upon which survival may once again depend.

Chiefs slept within the hulls of new canoes to invest them with *mana*. A story tells of a war party forced to escape back to sea after an unsuccessful landing. One chief had beached his canoe some distance from the others and was cut off; he reached it, but with neither time nor crew to launch it. Friends urged him to swim out to them, but he shouted, "Go! I will die here rather than abandon my canoe."

Smaller canoes used for fishing, surfing, and racing were of a single hull (*wa'a kekāhi*) with a stabilizing float of light weight wood. Now called "outriggers" because the float is rigged out from the hull, the float (*ama*) is carried on the left side of the hull throughout most of Polynesia. In a double-hulled canoe (*wa'a kaulua*), if hulls are not of equal length, the smaller hull rides on the left and is called the *ama*, and the larger hull the *'ākea*. Throughout Polynesia, crossbooms (*'iako*) connecting the hulls were made from straight poles, but in Hawai'i curved crossbooms were invented which held the center deck (*pola*) higher above the water, and gave greater strength. In groves of *hau*, a tree which produces naturally curving branches, canoe builders shaped the growth of young limbs with splints and ropes so the next generation might harvest perfectly formed crossbooms for double canoes. 70 feet seems to have been a typical length for a double canoe of a Hawaiian ruling chief. The greatest recorded hull length was 108 feet.

During the exploration of Polynesia, canoes venturing outward from the same center must have been of the same design; but when Europeans arrived many centuries later, regional differences in weather, seas, and available materials, as well as local cultural changes and inventions, had resulted in designs and ornament unique to each island group. Ships being as mortal as their makers, the earlier "archaic" design vanished as designs evolved which became "classical" to each island group. Except for pieces of preclassical Maori canoes excavated

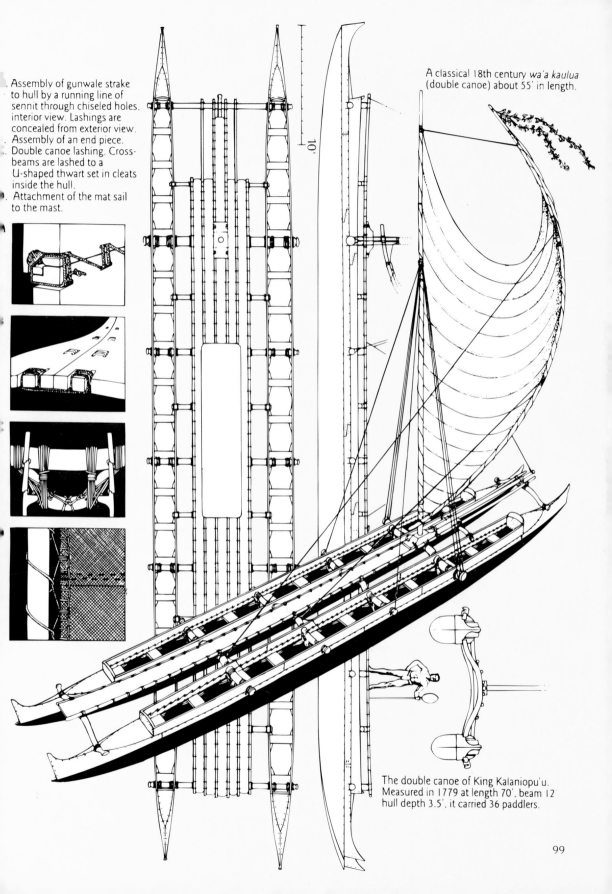

. Assembly of gunwale strake
to hull by a running line of
sennit through chiseled holes,
interior view. Lashings are
concealed from exterior view.
. Assembly of an end piece.
. Double canoe lashing. Crossbeams are lashed to a
U-shaped thwart set in cleats
inside the hull.
. Attachment of the mat sail
to the mast.

A classical 18th century *wa'a kaulua*
(double canoe) about 55' in length.

10'

The double canoe of King Kalaniopu'u.
Measured in 1779 at length 70', beam 12'
hull depth 3.5', it carried 36 paddlers.

99

on New Zealand, and pieces of an ancient seventy-foot canoe from a bog on Huahine, there is no hard evidence. Except for a petroglyph on Easter Island, and a 19th century Marquesan model said to be of an earlier design there is no descriptive record.

To develop a conjectural design for the ancient Polynesian voyaging canoe in order to depict it in paintings, the "age-distribution" method was used. Hull and sail design features, found to be most widely distributed throughout "Eastern" or "Marginal" Polynesia when Europeans arrived (including Hawai'i, the Marquesas, Tahiti, the Cook Islands and New Zealand) were taken to be most ancient because they must have been common features in the era of exploration and settlement. These also formed the functional basis for the author's design of the 1975 voyaging canoe replica *Hōkūle'a*, with the addition of some distinctively Hawaiian stylistic elements.

Long distance voyaging was made under sail, the distances being far too great for paddling. In Hawai'i, as long distance voyaging to the South Pacific declined, paddling replaced sailing as the major power mode for the shorter trips within the Hawaiian Islands. Chiefs prudently traveled with large numbers of bodyguards who, put to work as paddlers, provided freedom of mobility, the ability to move canoes against the wind or through calms. The shift to paddling brought a change in hull design from deep hulls that tracked well against the wind to shallower, round-bottomed hulls which were more maneuverable under paddles or sailing off the wind. Sails, no longer needed for working upwind, evolved to a full-bellied "crab claw" shape useful for running with the wind or on a broad reach.

The ancient, less specialized and more versatile triangular sail set on straight spars survived in the Marquesas, Tuamotus, Cook Islands and New Zealand, as well as in the sails of some Hawaiian fishing canoes. I used it on my first conceptual drawing for *Hōkūle'a*, but bowed to pressure to make the sails look "more Hawaiian." However, after years of experiment with sails cut to resemble the classical Hawaiian profile, the simpler, ancient triangular shape has proved to work more efficiently to windward or on a beam reach, and is now the sail that *Hōkūle'a* carries. Voyages between Hawai'i and Tahiti must be sailed slightly against the wind either way to overcome leeway.

No culture can long exist without its objects. The loss of an important object results in the loss of psychic as well as material benefits derived from it. Memory and meaning fades, and cultural disintegration occurs. Perhaps this is why canoes, as realities that link them to their ancestors, are still important to Pacific Islanders.

A FISHING CANOE OFF NORTH KONA
In the foreground a gannet dives for a flying fish. Forested Mount Hualalai rises to 8,200 feet in the background.
Although the scene is ancient, this view from the sea has not radically changed. Two popular resorts now stand on the
depicted shoreline: The Kona Village Resort and The Four Seasons Resort, Hualalai; but both are "low-rise" and
esthetically compatible with the landscape. *Collection of William and Diana Holland*

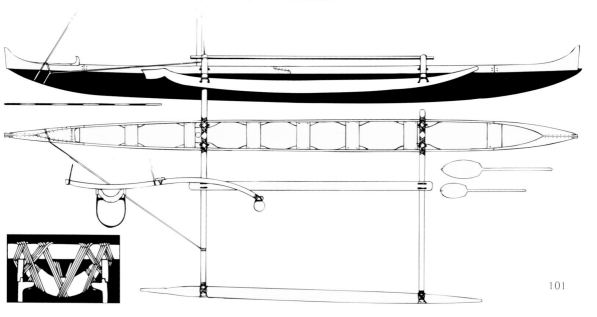

The Painting:

PERFORMERS

The dancers (*'ōlapa*) in the painting are wearing *kapa* garments of the style in use at the time of European contact (1778) as well as garlands of ferns. Their instruments are *'ulī'ulī*, rattles made from gourds and decorated with feathers. A *ho'opa'a* (drummer and chanter) at the extreme left is playing a *pahu hula* (dance drum). His companion plays the *pā ipu*, made of two gourds cemented together with breadfruit gum. Resonant sounds are produced in various rhythms by striking the sides with the fingers and the palm, and thumping the base upon a pad of folded *kapa*. Strapped to his thigh just above the knee is a *pūniu*, a small drum made from a coconut shell.

Above, a storyteller enchants his audience. Recitations of poems and chants, often by famous touring orators, drew enthusiastic and highly critical audiences.

At left is the *akua pā'ani*, a standard symbolic of Lonoikamakahiki, spirit of the Makahiki celebrations.

Collection of The Four Seasons Resort, Hualalai

PERFORMING ARTS

PERFORMANCES OF ORATORY, POETIC CHANTING, STORYTELLING, music, song and dance were created for religious purposes, to honor ruling chiefs and their family histories, and for entertainment. The *hula*, the most distinctive of the Hawaiian performing arts, involves dances accompanied by *mele* (music, song, and chanting).

The *hula* was performed by both men and women. Professional performers were trained in *hālau* (studios dedicated to the art) under the strict discipline of recognized *kumu hula* (teachers of the dance and associated arts), and were supported by chiefly patronage.

Patron spirits of the *hula* were Laka, Kapo, Pele and Hi'iaka—spirits also associated with forests and volcanoes. Performers danced for these spirits as well as for their mortal audiences. Rituals were conducted on the platforms of *heiau* dedicated to the *hula*, but the *hula* was not a part of the rites performed at other temples. Many amateurs, chiefs and commoners, practiced the art and performed together. King Kalani'ōpu'u would join his dancers with great glee, participating well into his eighties. A chief who didn't recognize him remarked, "This performance would be enjoyable if it were not for that silly old man."

At the birth of a high chief, a name chant would be composed and choreographed and the *hula* performed. *Hula* were composed to honor important chiefs and spirits, greet important visitors, commemorate important events and celebrate the scenic beauty of certain places. Chants that were not danced to (*oli*) were prayers, invocations for spiritual help, poetic recitations of legends, chants of praise for chiefs and heroes, and expressions of human response to life's mysteries. Veiled or hidden meanings (*kaona*) were frequently included—the life-giving rains of a certain place might be mentioned as an indirect reference to the sexual potency of its ruling chief. Gifted chanters with perfect inflection and voice control could stir deep emotions. Prolonged phrases could be chanted in one breath, often with a trill at the end. Some chants were traditional, requiring word-perfect delivery; others were spontaneously composed with embellishments to meet the expectations of the audience.

While some *hula* were for serious purpose, others were purely for entertainment. Some witnessed by early Europeans were grand performances involving many dancers and presented in several acts, while others were impromptu, performed by one or several dancers, sometimes singing, sometimes accompanied by chanters and instrumentalists.

In 1794, on Kaua'i, Captain George Vancouver witnessed a performance of three parts, *"... performed by three different parties consisting of about two hundred women in each..."* These were *"dressed in various coloured clothes, disposed with good effect"* and performed seated *"in five or six rows. In this situation and posture they exhibited a variety of gestures almost incredible for the human body so circumstanced to perform. The whole of this numerous group was in perfect unison of voice and action, that it were impossible, even to the bend of a finger, to have discerned the least variation. Their voices were melodious, and their actions as innumerable as, by me, they are indescribable; they exhibited great ease and much elegance."* The performance *" ... was conducted through every part with great life and vivacity; and was, without exception, the most pleasing amusement of the kind we had seen performed in the course of the voyage."*

Earlier, Vancouver had been less impressed by a *hula ma'i* (a dance praising by innuendo the genitals of a chief) which he found offensive and libidinous. Sex was a theme metaphorically expressed in dance, poetry, and song, especially during the Makahiki season—a time to celebrate the productive fecundity of the land, sea, and humans that derived from the union of male and female opposites. Makahiki was in full swing when David Samwell, with the Cook expedition, recorded the words to a song laden with sexual metaphor, *"...a song they* [Samwell's "dear girls"] *repeat in responses while dancing."*

Performers were of two classes: the *'ōlapa*, the younger, most agile dancers, and the *ho'opa'a*, those who sat or knelt in stationary positions, playing instruments and giving voice to songs.

Storytelling (*kūkahekahe*) and oratory (*ha'i'ōlelo*) at the most expert level must be included in the performing arts. At formal meetings between chiefs, orators often spoke for them with courtly speeches of welcome and praise. In the presentation of gifts between chiefs, an orator speaking on behalf of the giver might speak apologetically of an obviously fine gift as a humble thing, inadequate, but a sincere token of high esteem; whereupon the man speaking for the receiver would answer with high praise for the gift and the generosity of the giver.

Professional storytellers and poets entertained the communities they visited with sagas of a heroic past, long narratives of historical and legendary events which had been heard many times before but were much enjoyed with each retelling. Audiences were highly critical if any detail was omitted. The most popular storytellers were experts who could deliver narratives of many hours in length with dramatic flair, from word-perfect memories.

In 1830, the Queen Regent Ka'ahumanu, a pious convert mindful of the pleas of missionaries, banned public performances of the *hula*. Although the edict was flouted by some chiefs, the *hula* became a clantestine art, and training went underground under a nucleus of teachers who kept the art alive.

A public revival of the *hula* was approved by King Kalākaua for his coronation ceremonies in 1883, to the vociferous displeasure of the Calvinists. After the end of the Monarchy, *hula* again declined, many officials in the new government opposing it as "licentious." But the tradition was too much a part of the Hawaiian soul to be denied, and by the 1950s it was again flourishing.

Today, the Hawaiian performing arts, inspired as always by a few exceptionally talented leaders, is at the forefront of what has been called the Hawaiian Renaissance. As a living art form, the *hula* has a growing edge of innovation, both in the interpretation of the ancient traditions (*hula kahiko*) and in performances which employ 19th and 20th century costumes and music (*hula 'auwana*).

SPORTS AND GAMES

IT HAS BEEN SAID BY ROMANTICS WHO VIEW THE PEOPLE OF OLD as caring and sharing, motivated entirely by a spirit of *aloha* for each other, that competition was unknown—a notion far removed from the truth. By all accounts, competition was intense in politics, work, and in their arts and entertainments. Sports and games were fun, but spiced wherever possible with competitive interest. Their demise may be partly attributed to the influence of Christian missionaries, appalled at the fervor with which men gambled away their possessions on the outcomes. Nocturnal games of the kind played by groups of consenting adults also gave scandalized missionaries something to write home about.

But let's begin with the innocent games of childhood. There was *hei*, complicated patterns contrived by looping string around the fingers. Spinning tops were made from nut shells—the winner's top spun the longest. Balls of plaited *lauhala* were juggled to the timing of a song. *Pala'ie* was a ball and ring game; a ball, fixed with a cord to a stick with a loop at one end, was swung so it would strike the loop both from above and below in time to a song.

Foot racing (*kūkini*) involved sprinters and distance runners trained from childhood. Kites of various shapes were flown by all ages. Their fireworks was the spectacle of firebrands thrown from cliffs at night, thrilling audiences with the beauty of sparkling embers drifting in the

wind. Divers leaped from high cliffs into the sea.

Most sedentary was *kōnane*; similar to draughts or checkers, it was played on a flat stone or wooden board with pebbles of white coral and black lava, the places marked not by squares but by shallow pits in the board's surface. The objective was not to take all opposing pieces, but to be the one who could make the last move.

Bows and arrows were used to shoot rats. Cockfighting (*hākā-moa*) drew heavy betting; if the roosters were evenly matched it was a drawn battle, but if one ran off, its owner was the loser.

Ke'a pua was a Makahiki contest enjoyed by great numbers of men, women and children. Long darts, made from the dried flower stems and tassels of sugar cane, with tips weighted with dried earth, were hurled from a low mound to glance and ricochet along a smoothed course. Players wagered their darts on whose dart could slide the farthest.

'Ulu maika was a bowling game; stone disks, thrown to roll on edge, were aimed to pass between two stakes set at the end of a course. In *pahe'e*, spears or hardwood darts were thrown to slide for distance along a level course.

Surfing (*he'e nalu*) on surfboards or canoes was enjoyed by chiefs and commoners of both sexes. The wooden surfboards were shaped of *koa* or the much lighter *wiliwili*, or breadfruit, carefully smoothed and oiled. In competitions a buoy anchored in the shallows was the finish line. A Hawaiian invention, surfing is now universally popular.

The strongest paddlers were recruited for racing in *kialoa*, sharp and narrow canoes designed for speed. Both surfing and canoe races drew heavy betting among those on shore.

The element of gambling apparently led to canoe racing being shut down in the 19th century. Since its revival, however, it has flourished. Conducted and funded entirely by volunteer effort, it promotes values of teamwork and sportsmanship. During the racing season, young paddlers expend so much energy in their practice sessions that there is little left over for mischief. An international association includes clubs throughout the Pacific and Pacific Rim nations and is seeking acceptance as an Olympic event.

Boxing (*mokomoko*), wrestling (*hākōkō*), tug of war (*hukihuki*), spear throwing (*'ō'ō ihe*), and fencing with staves (*kākā lā'au*) were sports valued as training for war. There was also a martial art, *lua*, less a sport than a manner of hand-to-hand fighting that included sudden thrusting and leaping, bone-breaking, sparring with a spear—all with emphasis on self control and mental alertness.

Hōlua, a chiefly sport, involved launching a narrow sled with long wooden runners down a runway constructed of rockwork and paved with pebbles, over which a layer of some slippery thatching was laid. The longest known slide is Kaneaka in Keauhou, North Kona, Hawai'i. The lower half, which ended with the sledder flying into the sea, has been removed, but the slide was formerly a mile long. The remaining

upper half is fifty feet wide, in some places as much as eleven feet above the natural terrain, with only a few patches of pebble paving that have not been destroyed by cattle or shaken down among larger rocks by earthquakes.

There is no certain information on how the slide was thatched. An experiment by the writer proved that grass or leaves alone will not cushion sled runners from the lava pebbles underneath. The sled grinds to a sudden stop, while the rider continues forward, gathering cuts and bruises. However, it was found that a shingling of coarse *lauhala* mats covered with a scattering of grass will allow something close to terminal velocity. Old mats were abundant in Hawaiian houses as flooring underlayments and could be brought out and laid up quickly.

In the game of *no'a*, two groups would sit facing each other, with several bundles of *kapa* between them. A contestant passed his hand under the entire length of the bundles, and the opposing side would guess under which bundle he had dropped a small stone. The first side to accumulate ten points won.

'Ume might be termed a courtship game of the *maka'āinana*. Chanting a song, an umpire would walk among a nocturnal assembly of men and women. At a certain break in the song he would touch the nearest man with a wooden wand decorated with feathers. At the next break he would touch the nearest woman. The man and woman would go out into the night.

AFTERWORD

In 1995, when asked by Heather Cole, planner of the Kaʻupulehu Cultural Center at the Four Seasons Resort Hualalai, then under construction by the Hualalai Development Company, for ideas for paintings, I suggested something that had long been on my mind—a series in which each painting depicted a person of special rank or skill in the old culture. Eleven subjects were selected from the list presented. While writing captions for display with the paintings, I found that there was more that I wanted to say; hence, this little book.

That it presents a somewhat personal view is an unavoidable consequence of each person's view of the past being uniquely shaped by one's experiences and interests, resulting in differences of interpretation and emphasis. My focus on the canoe, for example, as the central object of the old culture, may not be shared by those whose interests lie in another cultural areas.

MAHALO!

Several friends were kind enough to plow through the manuscript in early drafts, including Lance Almon, Mel Kernahan, and Toni and Terry Wallace. A leading expert in Hawaiian language and culture, Fred Kalani Meinecke, Head of Hawaiian Studies at Windward Community College, Oahu, graciously advised me on questions of cultural history and the use of diacriticals in writing the Hawaiian language. James Raschick steered me through Pagemaker 6.5 and did most of the pre-press work. Such friends have saved me from more than a few errors and misjudgments. Those that remain are mine alone.

OTHER BOOKS BY THE AUTHOR:

VOYAGERS (Whalesong Publishing, 1991) One hundred forty of the author's paintings, drawings and sculpture in full color, with stories about the legendary and historical past of Hawai'i and the South Pacific. 176 Pages. Soft cover: $24.95 plus $3 Priority Mail. Hard cover: $29.95 plus $4 Priority Mail.

PELE, Goddess of Hawai'i's Volcanoes (Kawainui Press 1987, Revised, expanded 1997, Ancient traditions, folktales, and recent appearances of She Who Rules the Island of Hawai'i. Many full-color illustrations. $8.95 plus $3 Priority Mail.

Readers may write to: The Kāne Studio, Box 163, Captain Cook, Hawai'i 96704 or visit the Web Site: http://www.hitrade.com/Herb_Kane.html (e mail should include your postal mailing address)

SUGGESTED READING:

Beaglehole, J. C. 1967. *The Journals of Captain Cook on his Voyages of Discovery, Vol. III: The Voyage of the* Resolution *and* Discovery, *1776-1780*, Parts 1 and 2. Cambridge: Cambridge University Press (for the Hakluyt Society)

Handy, E. S. Craighill. 1927. *Polynesian Religion*. Bishop Museum Bulletin 34

Handy, E. S. Craighill and Elizabth Green Handy with Mary Kawena Pūku'i. 1972. *Native Planters in Old Hawai'i. Their Life, Lore and Environment*. Bernice P. Bishop Museum Bulletin 233

Handy, E. S. Craighill and Mary Kawena Pūku'i. 1972. *The Polynesian Family System in Ka'u, Hawai'i*. Rutland, Vt.: Charles E. Tuttle.

Ii, John Papa. 1959. *Fragments of Hawaiian History*. Honolulu: Bishop Museum Press

Kalākaua, David. *Legends and Myths of Hawaii*. Rutland, VT: Charles E. Tuttle.

Kamakau, Samuel Manaiakalani. 1961 *Ruling Chiefs of Hawai'i*. Honolulu: Kamehameha Schools Press.

_____. 1964. *Ka Po'e Kahiko*. The People of Old. Trans. Mary Kawena Pūku'i, ed. Dorothy Barrère. Honolulu: Bishop Museum Press.

_____. 1976. *The Works of the People of Old*. ed. Dorothy Barrère. Bishop Museum Special Publication 61. Honolulu: Bishop Museum Press.

_____. 1991 *Tale and Traditions of the People of Old: Nā Mo'olelo a ka Po'e Kahiko*.trans. Mary Kawena Pūku'i; ed. Dorothy Barrère

Kanahele, George He'eu Sanford. 1986. *Kū Kanaka, Stand Tall. A search for Hawaiian Values*. Honolulu: University of Hawai'i Press and Waiaha Foundation.

Kawaharada, Dennis (ed.). 1995 *Voyaging Chiefs of Havai'i*. Teuira Henry & Others. Honolulu: Kalamakū Press

Kelly, Marion. 1983. *Nā Māla o Kona: Gardens of Kona*. A history of land use in Kona, Hawai'i. Dept. of Anthropology Report 83-2; Bernice P. Bishop Museum. Honolulu: Bishop Museum Press.

Malo, David. 1951. *Hawaiian Antiquities*, trans. and ed. Nathaniel B. Emerson. Bernice P. Bishop Museum Special Publication no. 2

Pūku'i, Mary Kawena. 1983 *'Ōlelo No'eau: Hawaiian Proverbs and Poetical Sayings*. B.P. Bishop Museum Special Publication 71. Honolulu: Bishop Museum Press.

Pūku'i, Mary Kawena, E. W. Haertig, and Catherine A. Lee. 1979. *Nānā I Ke Kumu; Look to the Source*. Honolulu: Hui Hānai.

HERB KAWAINUI KĀNE (pronounced KAH-ney) is an artist-historian and author with special interest in Hawai'i and the South Pacific. Born in 1928, he was raised in Waipi'o Valley and Hilo, Hawai'i, and Wisconsin. He holds a masters degree from the Art Institute of Chicago. He resides in rural South Kona on the Island of Hawai'i.

Career experience began in the Chicago-Milwaukee area where, as an illustrator, he served clients in advertising, publishing and architectural design. Returning to Hawai'i in 1970, he worked as a design consultant on resorts in Hawai'i and the South Pacific and a cultural center in Fiji. After 1979 he limited his work to painting, writing, and sculpture. Clients include many private collectors, the Hawai'i State Foundation on Culture and the Arts, the National Park Service, *National Geographic*, and major publishers of books and periodicals. His art has appeared on postage stamps for the U.S. Postal Service and several Pacific Island nations.

Research on Polynesian canoes and voyaging led to his participation as general designer and builder of the voyaging canoe replica *Hōkūle'a*, which he served as its first captain. *Hōkūle'a* has now made five round trip voyages to the South Pacific including a 16,000 mile pan-Polynesia voyage to New Zealand, all navigated without instruments.

In 1984 he was elected a Living Treasure of Hawai'i. In the 1987 Year of the Hawaiian Celebration he was one of 16 persons chosen as *Po'okela* (champion). From 1988 to 1992 he served as a founding trustee of the Native Hawaiian Culture & Arts Program at Bishop Museum. He is the 1998 recipient of the Bishop Museum's Charles Reed Bishop Medal.